MW01030338

20 Hrs., 40 Min.

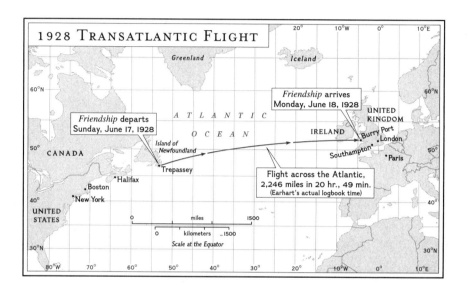

1928 TRANSATLANTIC FLIGHT

Greenland

Iceland

UNITED KINGDOM

Friendship arrives
Monday, June 18, 1928

A T L A N T I C

Friendship departs
Sunday, June 17, 1928

O C E A N

IRELAND

Burry Port
• London

Island of
Newfoundland

Southampton•

•Paris

CANADA

•Trepassey

Flight across the Atlantic,
2,246 miles in 20 hr., 49 min.
(Earhart's actual logbook time)

•Halifax

•Boston

•New York

UNITED
STATES

miles 1500

kilometers — 1500

Scale at the Equator

20 Hrs., 40 Min.

OUR FLIGHT IN THE *FRIENDSHIP*

THE AMERICAN GIRL, FIRST ACROSS THE ATLANTIC BY AIR, TELLS HER STORY

AMELIA EARHART

WITH AN INTRODUCTION BY ANTHONY BRANDT

NATIONAL GEOGRAPHIC
ADVENTURE CLASSICS

WASHINGTON, D.C.

Copyright © 2003 National Geographic Society.
Copyright © 1928 Amelia Earhart.
TM 2003 Amelia Earhart by CMG Worldwide Inc. www.cmgworldwide.com

Library of Congress Cataloging-in-Publication Data
Earhart, Amelia 1897-1937.
    20 hrs., 40 min: our flight in the Friendship/ Amelia Earhart.
      p.cm.
    ISBN 0-7922-3376-X
    1.Transatlantic flights. 2. Earhart, Amelia, 1897-1937. 3. Women air pilots—United
States—Biography I. Title.

    TL721.E3A3 2003
    629.13 092—dc21 [B]   2003042050

Illustration Credits: p.2, Corbis; p.7,Underwood & Underwood/Corbis; p.12, Bettmann/
Corbis; p.65, Underwood & Underwood/Corbis; p.117, 120,129, 134, 146, 151, 154, 164,
Bettmann/Corbis.

One of the world's largest nonprofit scientific and educational organizations, the National Geographic Society was founded in 1888 "for the increase and diffusion of geographic knowledge." Fulfilling this mission, the Society educates and inspires millions every day through its magazines, books, television programs, videos, maps and atlases, research grants, the National Geographic Bee, teacher workshops, and innovative classroom materials. The Society is supported through membership dues, charitable gifts, and income from the sale of its educational products. This support is vital to National Geographic's mission to increase global understanding and promote conservation of our planet through exploration, research, and education.

For more information, please call 1-800-NGS LINE (647-5463) or write to the following address:
NATIONAL GEOGRAPHIC SOCIETY
1145 17th Street N.W.
Washington, DC 20036-4688 U.S.A.

Visit the Society's Web site at www.nationalgeographic.com.

Contents

INTRODUCTION BY ANTHONY BRANDT

★

IN MAY 1932, five years after Charles Lindbergh's famous flight in *The Spirit of St. Louis*, Amelia Earhart became the second person—and the first woman—to fly the Atlantic Ocean solo. That summer she wrote something for *American Magazine* that summed up why she had taken the enormous risks the flight entailed and that caught nicely what sort of person she was. "Have you ever," she asked her readers, "longed to go to the North Pole? or smell overripe apples in the sunshine? or coast down a steep, snow-covered hill to an unknown valley? or take a job behind a counter selling ribbons, and show people how to sell ribbons as ribbons have never been sold before? or take a friend by the arm and say, 'Forget it—I'm with you forever'? or, just before a thunderstorm, to turn ten somersaults on the lawn?"

The North Pole. Friendship forever. *Ten* somersaults on the lawn. What shall we call it? Over the top exuberance? Sheer lust for life? She wrote poetry when the spirit moved her, bought her first plane (it had one of the first air-cooled engines; everybody advised her not to buy it, but within a couple of years air-cooled engines were the only ones anybody wanted) almost as soon as she learned how to fly. She asked to ride in the sidecar of one of the police motorcycles when she was being escorted from downtown to uptown New York because it looked like it would be a lot more fun than riding in the back of the limousine. On a train trip she rode in the locomotive for the same reason. She wanted to live with an intensity few of us can manage. Selling ribbons? She did, when she became famous, have her own line of clothing for a while and she took it seriously, becoming involved in all the design decisions. She was tall and slender and wore clothes well. Because she had thick ankles she wore pants, and made it fashionable to do so. She took Eleanor Roosevelt for a drive in her sporty little yellow convertible, which she called "The Yellow Peril" and which she always drove very fast. Eleanor was thrilled. She charmed Eleanor's husband, Franklin D. Roosevelt, the President of the United States, and used her influence with him both to promote aviation and to save the job of her lover, Gene Vidal (Gore Vidal's father), who was running the Bureau of Air Commerce at the time. She took Gene Vidal as a lover while she was married to the publisher George Palmer Putnam, but she had warned Putnam before they were married that she would not be bound, nor should he, by "any medieval code of faithfulness."

It wasn't that she was willful; rather it was that she was free. She was calm, fearless, cheerful in the face of life, and she attracted everybody. She lived for years in a settlement house, running programs for immigrant children, and considered herself more a social worker than an aviator, but that did not stop her from climbing up onto the roofs of buildings, which she liked to do. Flying her Kinner Airster one day, taking it up and up to see how high it would go, she inadvertently broke the women's altitude record. She was the main organizer of the Ninety-Nines, the first women pilots' organization. She had a big, wide smile and widely spaced gray eyes and short brownish-blond hair that she kept curled, but she was never cute. She had too much dignity to be cute. She believed that women should live lives rich in experience and have careers if they possibly could, and she lived her belief. She was a remarkable human being, a historic figure, one of those people who, skirting the farthermost edges of experience, open up possibilities for us all.

But you could not have predicted such a woman, leading such a life, from her years growing up. Indeed she was uncertain about what she wanted to do with her life for most of her first 25 or 30 years. She was born on July

24, 1897, in Atchison, Kansas, to a family that on her mother's side had a long history in Atchison and was locally quite prominent. Her father was trained as a lawyer but worked for railroads most of his life; he was an alcoholic, one of those who often manage long periods of sobriety, and he loved his children very much, but he led an unstable and peripatetic life. Amelia spent her early childhood living in Atchison with her maternal grandparents in the family home while her parents and sister lived in Kansas City, Kansas. Her charm was innate; she was always popular, always the center of a large circle of friends, and one could call her childhood in Atchison idyllic. But when she finally did join her parents on a permanent basis her life became like theirs, with her father moving from place to place, job to job. She attended six high schools in all, graduating by chance from one in Chicago.

Earhart herself seemed directionless. On a trip to Toronto in 1917 she saw some Canadian men who had been wounded in the First World War, and decided on the spot to become a doctor. In the meantime she volunteered to help and trained as a nurse's aide in the Spadina Military Hospital. It was there that she first took an interest in flying, watching Canadian aces fly at demonstrations and treating wounded airmen at the hospital and getting to know them. From there she moved to Massachusetts to be with her mother and sister, who was at a school in Northampton (her parents had separated). She learned how to repair automobile engines, a requirement for becoming an ambulance driver. Then she went to New York and enrolled in Columbia University's Extension Service, taking science courses and climbing—she could never be entirely serious—to the top of the dome of Low Library, the tallest spot on campus. But family obligations interrupted her academic career. Her parents had gotten back together, her father had taken a job in Los Angeles, and both parents wanted Amelia to be with them, so she quit Columbia and went to Los Angeles. She was 23 years old. She had yet to fly.

But even after she did start flying in 1921—after she had taken to it like the born pilot she was, bought her first airplane, learned how to do barrel rolls and loops and spins, even after she had become an attraction herself at the air shows and gained a certain amount of fame as a pilot— flying was not yet her life. She loved to fly and she was extremely good at it, but she was a complicated woman, she had high ideals, and she wanted more than just a life of flying; she wanted to serve, to be useful to the world.

She also had to make a living, for flying wasn't cheap. She worked for the telephone company as a clerk. She tried portrait photography in partnership with one friend, then got into the trucking business with another when photography didn't work out. She was elected to the Aviation Hall of Fame in 1923, but a year later she had sold her plane and drifted back East. She enrolled once more at Columbia, then dropped out, then tried Harvard, thinking about becoming a scientist, but taking only one course. After that she tried to get into MIT, thinking she might become an engineer. Nothing worked. She had no money, no prospects, and no idea of what to do about it. At the age of 29 she was reduced to applying for a job to the Women's Educational and Industrial Union in Boston, where she was living once again with her mother and sister, her parents having finally divorced.

It was then that she found social work. Someone at the WEIU sent her to Denison House, Boston's oldest settlement house, founded in 1892 along the lines of Jane Addams's Hull House in Chicago. Amelia talked her way into a job—and a way of life. Here, teaching English to immigrants and running programs for immigrant children, Amelia found herself. The work fulfilled the ideal of service she had set for herself and with her charm, her patience, and her smile she turned out to be ideally suited to the work. Within a year she was living at Denison House and, with her dynamism and ability, was beginning to attract attention once again. She was also still flying; she no longer owned a plane, but she rented one when she could and she stayed involved— she kept herself in the game. She wrote an article about aviation for a Boston magazine, and she flew in at least one air show. She was elected to the vice-presidency of the Boston chapter of the National Aeronautic Association, the first woman to become an officer of any chapter of the NAA anywhere.

That was in May 1928. It was the same month she was asked whether she wanted to be the first woman to fly the Atlantic Ocean—the flight that is the subject of this book.

* * *

It is a short book, and a modest one. She wrote it quickly, in a matter of weeks, and you would not know from it that the flight made her enormously famous despite the fact that she was only a passenger on board the Fokker tri-motor that crossed the ocean. But so, too, were all the other women vying for the honor of being the first woman to fly the Atlantic, just passengers, some of them mere publicity seekers with no experience at all of being the pilot of an airplane. Amelia Earhart's real accomplishments do not belong to this flight. Four years later she would fly that same ocean herself, alone, in a Lockheed Vega, and then set all kinds of other speed and distance records. Finally she would make the flight on which she vanished in the South Pacific—her flight around the world, traveling west to east, the flight that made her more than famous, that made her an immortal, a subject of endless fascination, a leather-jacketed ghost forever haunting the skies.

But it was still a very dangerous thing to fly the Atlantic Ocean. In the year after Charles Lindbergh flew the Atlantic, five other women had tried to make

the flight, all of them as passengers. Three of them had
died. That first year saw eighteen planes make the
attempt. Only three succeeded. Airplanes were a mere
quarter of a century old. The North Atlantic is famously
stormy, and fog banks are common. Weather reports
at that time were primitive and avigation was often
haphazard. The Fokker Amelia Earhart flew in was
made mostly of sheet metal; it rattled and roared like
an old steam engine. The cabin door had to be tied shut
with a small rope. The plane had been fitted up as a seaplane, with pontoons for safety, but pontoon design
was in its early stages; the pontoons were heavy, and the
trade-off was that you could get off the water ony if you
lightened the fuel load. When the plane landed just off
the coast of Wales, in the Bristol Channel, it was out
of gas. Dangerous? No question about it.

But Amelia fell asleep during the flight. That was
like her. She was always calm. She radiated calm. She
didn't talk about it, didn't brag about being fearless;
she just was. She writes with a light touch, she's self-
deprecating, funny about the delays, the difficulties they
faced. She makes the flight seem sporting, almost a lark.
She cracks jokes. What did people ask her afterward,
at all the banquets? "First: Was I afraid? Secondly: What
did I wear?" Rather than dwell on the danger
they faced she dwells on the beauty of the cloudscapes,
the loveliness of the stars at night, and when she has
to be serious she uses the space to promote aviation and
the safety of aviation, and she is careful to give credit

where credit is due. It's a short book, you can read it in an afternoon, but at the end of it you will be in love with her. You will adore her. And you will begin to understand what all the fuss was about.

She was truly special. The first Atlantic flight made it impossible for her to go back to Denison House to live, but she always considered herself first and foremost as a social worker. When someone asked her years later if she regretted not being a social worker anymore, she said she had never stopped working in the field. To herself she was not a hero. She was a flier who was using her fame to help women advance and to open opportunities for others. She vanished in 1937, nine years after the flight recorded here, and in a sense the glory days of aviation vanished with her. After her came World War II, jet planes, missiles, and the space race. Flying became common, something everybody does. Not until the astronauts did we have anyone like her, so gracious and casual, so brave, so beautifully heroic.

After she got back from her solo flight across the Atlantic in 1932 the American Woman's Association gave her a dinner and an award, and one of the speakers, Dr. Lillian Gilbreth, summed up her significance in a sentence. "Miss Earhart has shown us," she said, "that all God's chillun got wings."

Foreword by Amelia Earhart

In re-reading the manuscript of this book I find I didn't allow myself to be born.

May I apologize for this unconventional oversight as well as for other more serious ones—and some not so serious?

I myself am disappointed not to have been able to write a "work"—(you know, Dickens' Works, Thackeray's Works), but my dignity wouldn't stand the strain. I can only hope, therefore, that some of the fun of flying the Atlantic has sifted into my pages and that some of the charm and romance of old ships may be seen to cling similarly to the ships of air.

Introduction by Marion Perkins

✴

Miss Perkins is Head Worker at Denison House,
Boston's second oldest settlement, with which Amelia Earhart
has been identified for two years.

A TALL, SLENDER, boyish-looking young woman walked into my office in the early fall of 1926. She wanted a job and a part-time one would do, for she was giving courses in English under the university extension. Most of her classes were in factories in Lynn and other industrial towns near Boston. She had had no real experience in social work but she wanted to try it, and before I knew it I had engaged her for half-time work at Denison House. She had poise and charm. I liked her quiet sense of humor, the frank direct look in her grey eyes.

It was some time before any of us at Denison House knew that Amelia Earhart had flown. After driving with her in the "Yellow Peril," her own Kissel roadster, I knew that she was an expert driver, handling her car with ease, yes more than that, with an artistic touch. She has always seemed to me an unusual mixture of the artist and the practical person.

Her first year at Denison House she had general direction of the evening school for foreign-born men and women. She did little teaching herself, but did follow-up work in the homes, so necessary to the success of such an undertaking. In her report of her year's work after we had planned her next year's program, which did not include the evening school, she wrote: "I shall try to keep my contact with the women who have come to class; Mrs. S. and her drunken husband, Mrs. F.'s struggle to get her husband here, Mrs. Z.'s to get her papers in the face of odds, all are problems that are hard to relinquish after a year's friendship."

* * *

In the spring of 1927, Denison House was giving a country carnival for the benefit of the house. For such a good cause, Amelia consented to fly over Boston and drop publicity dodgers. She first said that she would do this if her name could be kept out of the papers! We had to use some persuasion to keep her from flying incognito. The first day of the carnival, the Boston police up and down Boylston and Tremont

Streets were perhaps too amazed to try to arrest a man
and woman, apparently Italian peasants just landed, who
drove back and forth in a queer yellow car, stopping
now and then to grind a tune on a battered hand-organ
and to distribute handbills.

The organ grinder was Amelia Earhart.

Youth, keeping a heart, a soul and a body that are
wide open to all the rich opportunities of life—that
is part of Amelia's creed. How many times I have
heard her say that, to her, one of the biggest jobs of
the social worker in a settlement is just that—to give
boys and girls the experiences that will keep them
young and that will develop a zest for life. Last fall,
she came to Denison House as a resident and as a
full-time staff worker. She has directed the work of
girls from five to fourteen years and has had general
charge of the pre-kindergarten. Jokingly we have
sometimes called Amelia the "official secretary,"
for she is the secretary of the staff, of the Board of
Directors (to which she was elected this year) and to
the House Committee of the board. She has an
unusual flair, in a meeting, for the gist of the
thought and expresses herself in writing with accuracy and originality. Last year and this, Amelia has
been a member of an inter-settlement committee
working on child-study records.

She herself made studies of children that show
her keen insight into child life. Here are sentences taken
from her record of a seven-year-old boy. "Ferris is fond

of making experiments of various kinds. How far can the pencil be moved before it falls? How high can the chairs be piled before spilling? He conceived the idea on a cold day of 'warming' his little sister's beads on his father's stove. That the beads were hot enough to burn the child when she put them on was not part of the experiment."

"Where is Miss Earhart now?" "Is she still flying?" "Gee, I hope she beats that other woman." These and hundreds of other questions greeted us on Tyler Street. "Is she coming back soon?" "I couldn't sleep last night thinking about her flying."

The day she told me of the trans-Atlantic project, and swore me to secrecy, she said, "And I'll be back for summer school. I have weighed the values and I want to stay in social work." Her simplicity, her honesty, her complete lack of any quality that makes for sensationalism—this is Amelia Earhart. A few days after the flight project was under way, a dinner guest at Denison House, who was learning to fly at the East Boston Airport, told of the big Fokker monoplane that Byrd was "to fly to the Antarctic"; just a quiet twinkle across the room to me from Amelia's eyes, and afterwards an infectious chuckle as we enjoyed the incident together.

One day last year, after a discussion of L. P. Jacks' lectures on The Challenge of Life, she handed me some verses. Here they are, more appropriate at this time than any words I can write:

Courage is the price that Life exacts for granting peace.
The soul that knows it not, knows no release
From little things:
Knows not the livid loneliness of fear,
Nor mountain heights where bitter joy can hear
The sound of wings.
How can Life grant us boon of living, compensate
For dull grey ugliness and pregnant hate
Unless we dare
The soul's dominion? Each time we make a choice, we pay
With courage to behold resistless day,
And count it fair.

CHAPTER I

TORONTO DAYS

THERE ARE TWO kinds of stones, as everyone knows, one of which rolls. Because I selected a father who was a railroad man it has been my fortune to roll.

Of course rolling has left its mark on me. What happened to my education is typical. Until the eighth grade I stayed the school year with my grandmother in Atchison, Kansas, and attended a college preparatory school. With the exception of two grades skipped, one spent trying a public school and one conducted at home under a governess-friend, my course was fairly regular—not including time out for travelling. However, it took six high-schools to see me through the customary four year course. Would it be surprising, considering this record, if I should come out with a right round "ain't" or "he done it" now and then?

Despite such risks there are advantages in a changing environment. Meeting new people and new situations

EARHART'S HIGH SCHOOL GRADUATION PORTRAIT

becomes an interesting adventure, and one learns to value fresh experiences as much as old associations.

When the war broke out for the United States I was at Ogontz School, near Philadelphia. My sister was at St. Margaret's College in Toronto and I went to visit her there for the Christmas holidays.

In every life there are places at which the individual, looking back, can see he was forced to choose one of several paths. These turning points may be marked by a trivial circumstance or by one of great joy or sorrow.

In 1918 Canada had been in the war four weary years—years the United States will never appreciate. Four men on crutches, walking together on King Street in Toronto that winter, was a sight which changed the course of existence for me. The realization that war wasn't knitting sweaters and selling Liberty Bonds, nor dancing with handsome uniforms was suddenly evident. Returning to school was impossible, if there was war work that I could do.

I started training under the Canadian Red Cross and as soon as possible completed the first-aid work necessary to qualify as a V.A.D. or nurse's aide. Those four men on crutches!

My first assignment was to Spadina Military Hospital, a rather small institution occupying an old college building converted for war use. Day began at seven and ended at seven, with two hours off in the afternoon. There were many beds to be made and trays and "nurishment" to be carried, and backs to be rubbed—some lovely ones!

Most of the men had been through a physical and emotional crisis. Many were not sick enough to be in bed and not well enough to find real occupation. Even when jobs were offered many lacked the mental stamina to take them—or make good at them, if taken. Spiritually they were tired out. Generally speaking they were a far harder group to care for than the really sick. For with the latter the improvements noted by the patient from day to day are cheerful mile posts, while these poor lads had lost even that means of happiness.

The first day I was in the hospital there was a fire. It was not serious enough for attendants to do anything but slam windows shut and stand by to carry out patients. Nearly everyone enjoyed the excitement except a few of the autumnal nurses and the poor fellows in the shell-shock ward. They suffered greatly for a few days from the effects of the unexpected disturbance which was to most of the other men a welcome break in their colorless existence.

Of course one of the jobs of a V.A.D. was to be a merry sunshine, not difficult for me whose I.Q. is low enough to insure natural cheerfulness. Despite our best efforts time often dragged. I wonder if we might not have accomplished more if we had all been good-looking and especially, perhaps, if we'd all worn brilliant colors instead of our grey and white uniforms. It's a pet theory of mine that color in a drab world can go a long way in stimulating morale. There's a suggestion, here, perhaps, for the management of the next war.

The monotony of the hospital prevailed with its food also. Even after ten years I am unable to look a jelly-roll in the eye. They were the diurnal diet in the officers' mess, just as rice puddings prevailed in the wards. I have a depressing memory of passing out little rice puddings in endless procession from the diet kitchen to the patients. Sometimes they came back untouched but bearing crosses and the inscription R.I.P. However, those who rated rice pudding were entitled to ice cream—if they could get it. We K.P.'s often did the getting for the patients most in need of cheer. Our funds were immorally collected, the winnings of matching pennies in the kitchen.

The war was the greatest shock that some lives have had to survive. It so completely changed the direction of my own footsteps that the details of those days remain indelible in my memory, trivial as they appear when recorded.

Days of routine slipped by quickly enough into months of nursing. I hope what we did was helpful. Somebody had to do it. There is so much that must be done in a civilized barbarism like war.

War followed one everywhere. Even entertainments weren't always merely fun. Often they meant having tea with a group of women who were carrying their war work into their homes. I remember, for instance, hours spent with a power sewing machine making pajamas.

The aviation I touched, too, while approached as

an entertainment was of course steeped with war. Sometimes I was invited to a flying field, Armour Heights, on the edge of the city. I think there were many planes there; I know there were many young pilots being trained—some very young. (As a matter of fact I wasn't exactly grey with age—twenty, then.)

But the planes were mature. They were full-sized birds that slid on the hard-packed snow and rose into the air with an extra roar that echoed from the evergreens that banked the edge of the field. They were a part of war, just as much as the drives, the bandages and the soldiers. I remember well that when the snow blown back by the propellers stung my face I felt a first urge to fly. I tried to get permission to go up, but the rules forbade; not even a general's wife could do so—apparently the only thing she couldn't do. I did the next best thing and came to know some of the men fortunate enough to fly. Among them were Canadians, Scotch, Irish and even Americans who could not pass our rigorous tests but were accepted in Canada at that time.

They were terribly young, those air men—young and eager. Aviation was the romantic branch of the service and inevitably attracted the romanticists. The dark side did not impress the enlisted men or me. To us there was humor in the big padded helmets, despite their purpose, which was to prevent scalp wounds in the crashes that were frequent in those days. The boys smeared their faces with grease, to prevent freezing, and that

IN FLIGHT GEAR, CA. 1925

seemed funny, too. The training planes were often under-powered, but no matter how well that was understood, the pilots joked about possible unpleasantness.

I have even forgotten the names of the men I knew then. But the memory of the planes remains clearly, and the sense of the inevitability of flying. It always seemed to me one of the few worth-while things that emerged from the misery of war.

I lived through the Armistice. Toronto was forty riots rolled into one that memorable day. Whistles awakened us. They blew continuously. Electric cars were stalled in the streets which were deep with trash. Insane old ladies crawled on top and hooked men's hats with their umbrellas. Fresh lads grabbed girls and powdered their faces with flour. Bands marched without knowing where they were going. There were speeches that were not heard and food that went untasted. Flags appeared everywhere, with confetti and streamers.

Those months in Toronto roused my interest in flying, although I did not realize it at the time. Perhaps it was the glamour of the environment, the times, or my youth. Aviation had come close to me.

CHAPTER 2

EARLY AVIATION

AT THE END of my brief hospital career I became a patient myself. It was a case of too much nursing, perhaps with too long hours, in the pneumonia ward. I picked up an infection and there followed several minor operations and a rather long period of convalescence.

At Toronto I had been put into the dispensary because I knew a little chemistry and because it appeared I was one of the few people who wouldn't drink the medical supply of whiskey. My brief experiences aroused my interest in medicine, and after the armistice I went to New York with the idea that I might become a physician. At Columbia I took up a very heavy course which included pre-medical work. Scholastically I think I could have qualified, but after a year of study I convinced myself that some of my abilities did not measure up to the requirements which I felt a physician should have.

My mother and father wanted me to come to Los Angeles. Regretfully I left New York and moved west.

Southern California is a country of out-door sports. I was fond of automobiles, tennis, horseback riding, and almost anything else that is active and carried on in the open. It was a short step from such interests to aviation and just then, as now, Southern California was particularly active in air matters.

I remember the first air meet I attended. It was near Long Beach, at Daugherty Field, the ocean side of the broad Los Angeles valley. The sky was blue and flying conditions were perfect, as I remember. As this was the summer of 1920 commercial flying was in its infancy. Even to go to see planes then was considered really sporting by the populace. There were mechanical imperfections of many kinds, but progress is made always through experimentation.

Certainly a great many of the people gathered that day had never before seen an aeroplane. The planes mostly were old war material, Jennys and Canucks. The Army and Navy were represented with the planes available at that time—Standards, D. H.'s, Douglasses, Martins, etc. None of the ships stand out distinctly in my mind as types. I imagine there were some bombing planes and pursuit jobs, but they all seemed to my untrained eye more or less routine two-seaters. Of course at that time I knew somewhat less than I do now.

However, one thing I did know that day. I wanted to fly. I was there with my father, who, I fear, wasn't having a very good time. As the dust blew in his eyes, and his collar wilted, I think his enthusiasm for aviation, such as it was, waned. He was slightly nonplussed, therefore, when I said:

"Dad, you know, I think I'd like to fly."

Heretofore we had been milling about behind the ropes which lined the field. At my suggestion we invited ourselves into the arena and looked about. I saw a man tagged "official" and asked my father to talk with him about instruction. I felt suddenly shy about making inquiries myself, lest the idea of a woman's being interested in trying to fly be too hilarious a thought for the official.

My father was game; he even went so far as to make an appointment for me to have a trial hop at what was then Rogers Airport. I am sure he thought one ride would be enough for me, and he might as well act to cure me promptly.

Next day was characteristically fair and we arrived early on the field. There was no crowd, but several planes stood ready to go.

A pilot came forward and shook hands.

"A good day to go up," he said, pleasantly.

My father raised an inexperienced eye to the sky and agreed. Agreeing verbally is as far as he went, or has ever gone, for he has not yet found a day good enough for a first flight.

The pilot nodded to another flyer. "He'll go up with us."

EARHART WITH ADMIRAL RICHARD BYRD AND

MRS. FREDERICK GUEST, SPONSOR OF THE FLIGHT

"Why?" I asked.

The pair exchanged grins. Then I understood. I was a girl—a "nervous lady." I might jump out. There had to be somebody on hand to grab my ankle as I went over. It was no use to explain I had seen aeroplanes before and wasn't excitable. I was not to be permitted to go alone in the front cockpit.

The familiar "contact" was spoken and the motor came to life. I suppose there must be emotion with all new experiences, but I can't remember any but a feeling of interest on this occasion. The noise of the motor seemed very loud—I think it seems so to most people on their first flight.

The plane rose quickly over some nearby oil der-
ricks which are part of the flora in Southern California.
I was surprised to be able to see the sea after a few
moments of climbing. At 2,000 feet the pilot idled the
motor and called out the altitude for me. The sensation of speed is of course absent, and I had no idea of
the duration of the hop. When descent was made I know
the field looked totally unfamiliar. I could not have
picked it out from among the hundreds of little squares
into which populated areas are divided. One of the
senses which must be developed in flying is an acute-
ness in recognizing characteristics of the terrain, a
sense seldom possessed by a novice.

Lessons in flying cost twice as much in 1920 as they
do now. Five hundred dollars was the price for ten or
twelve hours instruction, and that was just half what had
been charged a few years before.

When I came down I was ready to sign up at any
price to have a try at the air myself. Two things deterred
me at that moment. One was the tuition fee to be
wrung from my father, and the other the determination to look up a woman flyer who, I had heard, had
just come to another field. I felt I should be less self-
conscious taking lessons with her, than with the men
who overwhelmed me with their capabilities. Neta
Snook, the first woman to be graduated from the
Curtiss School of Aviation, had a Canuck—an easier
plane to fly than a Jenny, whose Canadian sister it
was. Neta was good enough to take payments for time

in the air, when I could make them, so in a few days I began hopping about on credit with her. I had failed to convince my father of the necessity of my flying, so my economic status itself remained a bit in the air.

I had opportunity to get a fair amount of information about details of flying despite my erratic finances. In Northampton, where I had stayed a while after the war, I had taken a course in automobile repair with a group of girls from Smith College. To me the motor was as interesting as flying itself, and I welcomed a chance to help in the frequent pulling down and putting together which it required.

New students were instructed in planes with dual controls; the rudder and stick in the front cockpit are connected with those in the rear so that any false move the student makes can be corrected by the instructor. Every move is duplicated and can be felt by both flyers. One lands, takes off, turns, all with an experienced companion in command. When passengers are carried these controls are removed for safety's sake with little trouble. If there is a telephone connection, communication and explanation are much easier than by any methods of signs or shouting. This telephone equipment, by the way, seems to be more usual in England than here.

I am glad I didn't start flying in the days of the "grass cutters," which exemplified an earlier method of flying instruction. One of the amusing sights of the war training period was that of the novices hopping about the countryside in these penguin planes. They could fly only a few feet from the ground and had to be forced off to do that. The theory had been that such activity offered maximum practice in taking off and landing. In addition it was a sort of Roman holiday for the instructors—they had nothing much to do but, so to speak, wind up their playthings and start them off. And nothing very serious could happen one way or the other.

It was really necessary for a woman to wear breeks and leather coats in these old days of aviation. The fields were dirty and planes hard to enter. People dressed the part in a semi-military khaki outfit, and in order to be as inconspicuous as possible I fell into the same styles. A leather coat I had then, I wore across the Atlantic, eight years later.

Neta sold her plane and I bought one and changed instructors after a few hours' work. John Montijo, an ex-army instructor, took charge of me and soloed me after some strenuous times together. I refused to fly alone until I knew some stunting. It seemed foolhardy to try to go up alone without the ability to recognize and recover quickly from any position the plane might assume, a reaction only possible with practice. In short, to become thoroughly at home in the air, stunting is as necessary as, and comparable to, the ability to drive an automobile in traffic. I was then introduced to aerobatics and felt not a bit afraid when sent "upstairs" alone for the first time.

Usually a student takes off nonchalantly enough but

AMELIA EARHART IN A PHOTOGRAPH TAKEN SHORTLY
BEFORE THE *FRIENDSHIP* FLIGHT

doesn't dare land until his gas supply fails. Any field
is familiar with the sight of beginners circling about
overhead, staying up solely because they can't bear to
come down. The thought of landing without their
instructors to help them, if need be, becomes torture,
which is only terminated by the force of gravity.

In soloing—as in other activities—it is far easier to
start something than it is to finish it. Almost every
beginner hops off with a whoop of joy, though he is
likely to end his flight with something akin to D. T.'s.

I reversed the process. In taking off for the first
time alone, one of the shock absorbers broke, causing
the left wing to sag just as I was leaving the ground. I

didn't know just what had happened, but I did know something was wrong and wondered what I had done. The mental agony of starting the plane had just been gone through and I was suddenly faced with the agony of stopping it. It was all in a matter of seconds, of course, and somehow I contrived to do the proper thing. My brief "penguin" flight came to a prompt conclusion without further mishap.

When the damage had been repaired, I took courage to try again, this time climbing about 5,000 feet, playing around a little, and returning to make a thoroughly rotten landing. At once I had my picture taken by a gentleman from Iowa who happened to be touring California and wanted a few rare sights for the album back home.

CHAPTER 3

My Own Plane

IN THE WAR some students were soloed with as little as four hours' training. That meant they were considered competent to go up in their planes alone after this amount of instruction. Obviously these were exceptional students. In civilian flying, ten or twelve hours, I imagine, would be about the minimum training. But these hours usually mean simply routine instruction in straight flying, comparable to the novice driving his automobile along the level uncrowded country highway. For the auto-mobilist beginner the problem comes when he first meets traffic, and a big truck, say, suddenly cuts in ahead of him. Can he handle the emergency, or will he crash? And what will the beginner do when his car, or the other fellow's, skids on the wet pavement for the first time? The answer is that good driving results from experience and the requisite of having met many varied situations.

And so with planes. Straight flying is, of course, the necessary basis; but it is the ability to meet crises, large and small, which counts. And the only way to train for that is, as I have said, to have actual instruction in stunting and in meeting emergencies. To gain experience after the beginner has soloed, and while he is at home in a plane he knows intimately and upon a field familiar to him, he should play around in the air for four or five hours alone, practising landings, take-offs, turns and all the rest of it where he is perfectly safe and can come down easily any time.

Then he should have three or four more hours' instruction in emergency situations. This feature is too often overlooked. As I visualize it, the beginner should go up with an instructor with dual controls again and should get himself into—and out of—one scrape after another, including forced landings. After he has done so repeatedly, he will have confidence and a real feeling of what must be done, and done instantly, under any given set of circumstances. More of this sort of follow-through training and there would probably be fewer of the accidents which too often are beginners' bad luck.

I had rolled up the tremendous total of two and one-half hours' instruction when I decided that life was incomplete unless I owned my own plane. Those were the days of rather heavy, under-powered ships which lifted themselves from the ground with a lumbering effort. The small sport planes were just beginning to appear, most of them in experimental stages. The field where I flew was owned by W. G. Kinner of the Kinner Aeroplane and Motor Corporation, who was then developing one of the first sport planes made.

I watched that plane at work in those days when I was cutting my aviation eye teeth. Little by little I became able to distinguish the different makes of planes, and the finer points of their performance. I realized that the small plane took off more quickly, climbed more steeply, was faster and easier to handle than its bigger brothers with their greater horse power and wing spread.

After two and one-half hours I really felt myself a competent judge of planes! A few hundred solo hours since then have modified greatly that initial self-confidence! The fact that wise pilots with a thousand hours or so warned me against this little fellow, influenced me not. I wanted that sport plane that hopped off like a sandpiper and actually seemed to like it. And I set about buying it. My pilot friends came to me quietly. "Look out for the motor," they said. Power was the thing, they assured me, and the paltry 60 horse power of the little Lawrence air-cooled motor simply didn't measure up to commonsense requirements. It is interesting to realize that the plane in which Lady Heath made her famous solo flight from Croydon to South Africa and back, the lovely little Avian which I bought from her, actually has little more horse power than this first love of mine.

The small air-cooled motor I speak of was the first in this country. The man who had built it was not well

known then. He was one of a number of able experi-
menters who were working out their own private ideas,
often in the face of all sorts of sacrifices. The name of
the builder of this original air-cooled engine is Charles
L. Lawrence, famous today as the creator of the Wright
Whirlwind which carried Lindbergh, Byrd, Chamberlin,
Maitland and others on their famous flights, and with
which our own *Friendship* was equipped.

The idea of an air-cooled engine appealed to me.
The elimination of the water cooling system meant
simplification and a notable decrease in weight. Thanks
largely to the lightness of the engine and resulting light
plane, it was possible for me to pick it up by the tail and
move it around the field easily, whereas with the Canucks
and the others it took at least a man, or a dolly, and great
effort. I was won by the motor, despite some weaknesses,
and I have never regretted that first enthusiasm. So I said
"no" to my pessimistic pilots, and "yes" to Mr. Kinner.

The price was $2000. After talking it over with my
father he agreed that I needed the plane and that I
should have it, and promised to help out in paying for
it. But I am afraid my salesmanship was faulty for he
did not stay "sold." I signed the sales contract and
plunked down all my available capital to seal the bar-
gain before I knew of his indecision. Consequently,
there wasn't any backing out even if I had wanted to—
which I emphatically did not.

To pay for that plane I got the first job I ever had,
the telephone company taking me on as unskilled

labor. I was associated with the office boys at the back of the office, an association which I was told was one of the worst in the organization. We did things to the mail, opened it, sorted it, distributed it. I also filed letters and then tried to find them again. I liked the job and the boys, who were very funny and not the criminals they were pictured.

Perhaps this move on my part doesn't seem very convincing, for obviously my salary as playmate of office boys would have to run on for a long time before it would wipe out the balance of the $2000. But it did help my credit immensely! I think it made my flying companions believe I was in earnest.

It also affected mother to the extent that she finally wiped out my indebtedness, on condition I resign and stay home a little. By the way, *she* has remained sold, and it was her regret she wasn't with me on the trans-Atlantic flight, if I would go.

There was a partnership of interest, and of near poverty, between many of us in those days. Aviation demanded much from its devotees—and there was plenty of opportunity for sacrifice. Many pioneers sank their teeth into aviation's problems at the very beginning—or was it the other way about?—and simply wouldn't let go.

So I owned my own plane. Immediately I found that my whole feeling toward flying had changed. An added confidence and satisfaction came. If I crashed, it was my own responsibility and it was my own property that was being injured. It is the same sort of feeling that obtains, I think, in driving. There is a freedom in ownership which is not possible with a borrowed car.

Of course I had shouldered a new responsibility. I had an expensive, inanimate object on my hands. I wanted it to look all right on the outside and *be* all right on the inside. Few words are more expressive than "care and upkeep." Fortunately in their obligations I was remarkably lucky. The plane was an experiment for Kinner, a model for production. Obviously he wanted to have demonstrated exactly what it could do. When I was around, I was informally a sort of demonstrator— we agreed that he could use it for demonstration in return for free hangar space, and I was given much mechanical help, and other assistance in addition to hangar space. It was this situation, I suppose, which really made it possible for a "telephone girl" to carry on. At any rate, to me the important fact is, that I secured many free hours in the air and much kindly help.

Demonstrating has other advantages: it means an effort to sell someone something. And selling involves debating the virtues of the thing to be sold, the prospective purchaser usually being on the silent end of the debate. So I found myself studying the virtues of my plane, and in so doing, those of others.

The first thing most people want to do when they get a new car is to take someone out driving in it; a desire which seems to apply equally to a plane. Somehow I have always felt a little differently. It isn't that I am not proud of my possession, but that I always have a suspicion that my pride may run away with my prudence. If it be car or plane, my inclination is to be absolutely sure of myself before I whisk anybody else's body around in it. Consequently my air passengers were few.

As a matter of fact, I have never asked any men to take a ride. I think I have always feared that some sense of gallantry would make them accept, even though they did not trust me. So my male passengers have always had to do the asking.

There were plenty of potential joy riders around the fields in those days. Many of them had drifted into aviation after the war—or rather had not drifted out. They wanted to be near planes, and accepted any opportunity to take a ride no matter who the pilot or what the machine. From this gang have graduated many of the men who are today the real working human backbone of the industry.

From them were recruited the gypsy flyers who barnstormed their way around the country and whose activities actually figured largely in the development of American aviation. It was they who kept alive public interest. Mostly they flew wrecks, old war crates tied together with baling wire. Anything that would get off the ground—most of the time—was good enough for them. Many of them, of course, paid a heavy price for their devotion.

For me flying was a sport and not a circus—I used to sneak away to a secluded field and practise, with no one to bother. I appeared in public only on special occasions. For instance once I was invited to take part in a meet held by the Aero Club of Southern California at Pasadena. It was purely a public demonstration, a sort of circus, yet it was for a purpose—to raise money for the Club and to arouse local interest in flying.

I was asked to do a little stunting, the usual thing on occasions of this kind. The little plane looked well in the air, so I accepted. The minute I flew up to the field I began to feel like a clown, although happily there were two of us female freaks to divide the honors and the odium.

There was plenty of chatter about two "aviatrixes," but the chatterers never knew that they came near having something actually to talk about. For, as I reached the field, after flying from my own hangar, a spark plug blew out. Luckily I was over the field just then as otherwise I might have made my landing in a treetop. One cylinder dead in eight is not so serious a matter as one in three. I had only three and wished for eight just then.

It happened that my own engine was on the repair bench and the boys at the field, determined to get me to the meet, had worked all night switching the motor from the Goodyear pony blimp over to my plane. In the blimp the motor had been run at a low speed and as a result when I turned it up to my requirements one of the spark plugs could not stand the strain. After a new extra long plug was inserted I started out again.

It was a beautiful day with splashes of clouds which sailed up over the mountains from the desert westward.

They made a perfect background for the audience below and a perfect playground for anyone in the sky. Speaking seriously, the most effective stunting, from an artistic point of view, should be staged against just such a sky. Alternate white and blue with irregular outline brings out the full grace of the maneuvering plane.

A good deal of air racing was going on then all over the country. But my feeling toward it was similar to my feeling toward any other public flying. It was not for me. I wasn't good enough. I remember one funny offer. A group of people wanted to stage a race and seemed to think that I was timid about entering. So they suggested that I let their own pilot fly most of the race, then come down and let me get aboard, out of sight of the audience, and finish up as the "lady flyer" who had piloted the plane to victory.

Another proposal I remember.

"How would you like to make some easy money?" I was asked.

"How?"

"Bringing some stuff across the border."

Stuff—liquor, aliens or dope?

"Liquor?" I guessed.

My philanthropic friend shrugged his shoulders. "A woman can get by where a man can't. No one would ever suspect you. There's not a thing to be afraid of. You could do it easy."

It was a pretty compliment, but I declined.

One day I went up with my plane to establish its ceiling—that is, to see how high it would go.

There is a point in altitude beyond which, of course, a given plane cannot climb, just as with automobiles, there is a limit to the grade that can be negotiated and a speed that can be attained. In flying, an added factor is entailed, in the rarification of atmosphere with height, which affects plane, motor and personnel.

To make the record official I asked the representative of the Aero Club of Southern California to seal my barograph. This instrument records altitude in ink on a revolving drum. When sealed it is impossible for the flyer to alter it.

It was a good day and I climbed easily for about 13,000 feet. Thereafter I began to have trouble. My spark control lever became disconnected and I could not regulate the spark in my engine. As a result a terrific vibration and knocking started. I thought the engine would jump out of its frame. There wasn't anything to do but come down, although I was still climbing fifty feet a minute.

As soon as the official read my barograph there was great rejoicing, for apparently I had established a woman's altitude record. The news got in the papers. One clipping read:

> Miss Amelia Earhart, local aviatrix, established a new altitude record for women yesterday under the auspices of the Aero Club of Southern California.

Flying her own Kinner Airster, containing a 60-foot power motor, she ascended more than 14,000 feet.

Her sealed barograph registered little vibration until about 12,000 feet, where Miss Earhart said something went wrong with the motor. At the time she was climbing easily, about 50 feet a minute, which would have continued perhaps for several thousand feet more if the engine difficulty had not arisen.

Although my figure of 14,000 feet was not extraordinary, the performance of my engine was interesting. With the little Lawrence power plant of less than 60 h.p. I had gone up much farther than some of the higher powered planes which should have been more efficient.

A little while later I made another attempt. The weather was pretty good at the start. At 10,000 feet I ran into clouds. At 11,000 feet sleet, and at about 12,000 feet dense fog. This was an entirely new experience, and very disquieting. For the first time in my life, I had that strange feeling experienced by the flyer in fog.

Under such circumstances it is impossible to tell what the plane is doing. It may be upside down or turning giant circles. Without instruments the pilot simply does not know his position in space—there are no outside landmarks with which to check. Of course, if one is really upside down for any length of time one's feet drop back from the rudder and the safety belt tightens; or if in a skid a side blast of wind gives a belated warning, etc.

It was extraordinarily confusing and, realizing I could not go farther, I kicked the ship into a tail spin and came down to 3000 feet where I emerged from the fog and landed.

I remembered one of the old-timers came up and looked at my barograph record. His eyes fixed on a vertical line just before the record ended. "What does that mean," he asked. "Did you go to sleep along in there?"

I told him about getting out of the fog by way of a tail spin.

He certainly wasn't impressed favorably.

"Suppose the fog had lasted all the way to the ground?" he asked.

I bring this experience up because of its important bearing both on the training of pilots and on flying in general; especially schedule flying. It is immensely important for a pilot to learn to fly by instruments, as distinct from flying "by horizon." The night flyer or the navigator in fog must depend upon his instruments to keep his course, equilibrium and altitude. It did not require the flight of the *Friendship* through long hours of fog and cloud to teach me the profound necessity of this.

CHAPTER 4

EAST TO BOSTON

★

CRASHES WERE FREQUENT enough in these earlier days.
I had one myself, during my instruction period. Owing
to carelessness in not refuelling, the motor cut out on
the take-off, when the plane was about 40 or 50 feet in
the air. Neta Snook was with me, but she couldn't help
depositing us in a cabbage patch nearby. The propeller
and landing gear suffered and I bit my tongue.

The crash was an interesting experience. In such
a crisis the passage of time is very slow. I remember it
seemed minutes while we were approaching the
inevitable cabbages, although of course it was only a few
seconds. I had leisure to reach over and turn off the
switch before we hit.

More than once I have nosed over. Whenever a
plane is compelled to stop suddenly there is danger of
so doing. I have come down in a muddy field where the
wheels stuck. On one occasion I landed in a mattress of

dried weeds five or six feet high which stopped me so suddenly that the plane went over on its back with enough force to break my safety belt and throw me out. These are the flat tires of flying and are only as incidental. But real trouble did come to my plane eventually.

I had decided to leave Los Angeles and to sell it, much as I disliked the parting. A young man who had done some flying during the war liked the little sandpiper and eventually purchased it.

After the new owner took possession the first thing he did was to ask a friend to go up with him. At a few hundred feet he began some figure eights, banking vertically and working between a gas station and a telegraph pole. All on the field stood rooted to the spot. They knew what chances he was taking. As I remember it, Kinner sent for an ambulance. Suddenly, on one vertical bank the plane slipped. That was the end of it. Both men were killed. It was a sickening sort of thing because it was so unnecessary.

I lingered on in California, another sunkist victim of inertia—or was it the siren song of the realtors? I bought a new plane. Or rather I collected it, because I found I could not buy it all together. At this time there were few who believed that an air-cooled motor for planes would become practical. Human nature normally condemns anything new. The complaint of many pilots was that a multiple cylinder radial motor would be too clumsy to sit on the nose of a plane and would cause too much "head resistance." So why bother with one or two cylinder motors which developed little power comparatively? Kinner had a dream. He built one of his own. It had been bought by the man who financed one of the first planes built, in the west, by Donald Douglas, designer of the Round the World Cruisers. Mr. Davis and Mr. Douglas at the time were planning a trans-continental non-stop hop, using a big Liberty engine. But the P.2 flown by Macready and Kelly to San Diego, in the first coast to coast flight, got across first. I bought the Kinner engine from Davis, who was not ready to use it just then. It was the first engine that Kinner turned out.

Of course it was full of "bugs"—no degree of mechanical perfection is ever attained without successive stages of development. Each improvement is a result of many practical working tests. Human intelligence seems to grasp ideas in steps and must work through complicated details to efficient simplicity. The first automobiles had whip holders on the dash, remember. The planes and motors which we see today are the results of evolution. There was a preliminary design of the now famous Wright Whirlwind motor as early as 1917 and it, in turn, had grown from models of air-cooled radials begun by Mr. Lawrence in 1914.

The greatest pleasure I found in my experience with Kinner's motor was that of perhaps having a small part in its development. Its many little ailments had to be diagnosed and cured later. It smoked and spattered oil. Adjustment of a proper propeller was difficult. One of its eccentricities was an excessive vibration which tickled the soles of the feet when they rested on the rudder bar, putting a new meaning into joy ride. Such was the hilarious beginning of one of a group of motors which are being developed in the United States.

The idea of returning to the east, and doing it by air, had been simmering in my mind. Maps and data were all pretty well prepared. Then the old infection, incurred in the Toronto Hospital work, returned, and I was forced to abandon the hop, to the satisfaction of my parents.

My health was so precarious that, disappointed in my intention to fly, I exchanged my plane for a car and drove across the continent. Mother went with me to remind me I was too ill to fly, and together we covered more than 7000 miles before we reached Boston.

I enjoyed three days in Boston before entering Massachusetts General Hospital for a short stay. After convalescing a while I set off for New York, to re-enter Columbia. The next summer was spent at Harvard and the following autumn I began to look about for a job. My sister was teaching, so I indulged in it too. Teaching and settlement work filled the following years—filled them very full, for both occupations require much of one's life. All these other activities allowed little or no time for aviation.

Inevitably certain contacts had persisted from the California days so it was no surprise to hear from Mr.

Kinner. He asked me whether I knew anyone in Boston who would take the agency for his planes and motors. I dropped in on the Chamber of Commerce for information. It was evident from the facts gathered from Bernard Wiesman, secretary of the committee on aviation, that the town could struggle along for a while without the additional luxury of a new plane. The air-mail industry seemed to be as strong a dose of aviation as Boston could stand at the time, and Sumner Sewall was having to hold her nose while he spooned that in.

I joined the Boston chapter of the National Aeronautic Association as a reawakening of my active interest in aviation. Ultimately I was made Vice-President (perhaps to get rid of me) serving under Mr. Sewall. Subsequently his activities took him to New York and when I returned from the trans-Atlantic flight I found myself the first woman President of a body of the N. A. A.

Several months later Mr. Kinner wrote again and said he himself had found an agent, who would communicate with me. The hand of Allah had thrown Harold T. Dennison, a young architect of Quincy, in Mr. Kinner's way in California. Mr. Dennison came home determined to build an airport. He owned enough land for an emergency field on the marshes from which Beachey flew to Boston Light in 1910 to win $10,000.

I gathered a few dollars together and became one of five incorporators of a commercial aeronautical concern. Today Dennison Aircraft Corporation is

MRS. FREDERICK GUEST, SPONSOR OF THE *FRIENDSHIP*
FLIGHT, STANDS AT LEFT WITH LOUIS "SLIM" GORDON,
EARHART, WILMER STULTZ, AND MRS. FOSTER WELSH

working to create a commercial airport adjoining the
naval air base at Squantum.

There is so much to be done in aviation and so much
fun to be got from it, that I had become increasingly
involved before the flight of the *Friendship*. I was busy,
too, with Miss Ruth Nichols of Rye in trying to work
out some means of gathering more women into the
fold. The National Playground Association had asked
me to be on their Boston committee and judge in the
model airplane tournament they were sponsoring in
September, 1928. The tournament combined my two
greatest interests, aviation and social work, in an

unusual way, and I was very glad to serve. Unfortunately the social worker became submerged in the aerial joy-rider and the latter has been too much occupied since her return to be of any use whatsoever.

CHAPTER 5

PREPARATIONS

WHEN IT WAS ALL OVER I read in the papers that I had
been planning a trans-Atlantic flight for a year. I
read much else that was equally imaginative. In fact,
the press introduced me to an entirely new person. It
appeared that I was a demi-orphan; my father, I
learned, had been dead four years—I saved that clipping for him. One day I read that I was wealthy, the
next that the sole purpose of my flight was to lift the
mortgage from the old homestead—which there isn't
any—I mean homestead.

The truth about the chance to fly was as amusing as the
journalistic scenarios. The opportunity came as casually as
an invitation to a matinee, and it came by telephone. As
a matter of fact, the three of us who made the Atlantic crossing together all were similarly collected by telephone.

Commander Byrd telephoned Stultz, suggesting
the possibility. Stultz then communicated, by telephone again, with those organizing the flight. Tentative

arrangements were made as regarded himself. They asked him to choose his flying mechanic. On April 7, via long distance telephone, he reached Slim Gordon, then at Monroe, La., with the "Voice of the Sky" Corporation. "Meet me at the Cadillac Hotel in Detroit on the 9th, if you want to fly the Atlantic." "Sure," said Gordon.

So next morning Slim serviced his ship; told the boys he wasn't taking off with them that day and left to keep his appointment.

It was settled in no time at all—certainly within the limits of the conventional three minute telephone conversation.

As for me, I was working as usual around Denison House. The neighborhood was just piling in for games and classes and I was as busy as could be. I remember when called to the phone I replied I couldn't answer unless the message was more important than entertaining many little Chinese and Syrian children. The word came assuring me it was.

I excused myself and went to listen to a man's voice ask me whether I was interested in doing something aeronautic which might be hazardous. At first I thought the conversation was a joke, and told the gentleman so. At least twice before I had been approached by bootleggers who promised rich reward and no danger—"absolutely no danger to you, Leddy."

The frank admission of risk piqued my curiosity and I enquired how and why I had been called.

I demanded references and got them. They were

good references, too. After checking up, I made an appointment for late the same day.

"Should you like to fly the Atlantic?"

Such was the greeting when I met Hilton H. Railey who had done the telephoning.

He told me, without mentioning specific names, that Commander Byrd's tri-motored Fokker had been purchased and was destined for trans-Atlantic flight. He asked me if I would make the flight if opportunity offered. Then he told me that a woman owned the plane, and had intended flying it herself. Circumstances had just arisen which made it impossible for her to go but there was a chance that another woman might be selected in her place; and Mr. Railey had been asked by George Palmer Putnam, New York publisher, to help find such a person.

Then followed the first period of waiting. I did not know whether or not I was going. I didn't know whether the flight really would come off. I didn't know whether I should be selected if it did. And in the meanwhile I was asked to clear the decks so I could get off if the opportunity actually arose.

At Denison House we were just working out our summer plans, with me in charge of the summer school. If I actually was to leave, Marion Perkins, our head worker, must get someone for my place. So the chaos of uncertainties spread in ripples out from me as a center.

I think what troubled me most just then was the difficulty of my relations, under the circumstances, with all these people whose plans were so much dependent upon my own. Yet I was pledged to secrecy and could not say a word to them. And of course, it is rather disconcerting to carry on a job at a desk, or with settlement children, with the probability of a trans-Atlantic flight pending.

In ten days or so I was asked to go to New York. There I met David T. Layman, Jr., who, with Mr. John S. Phipps, talked things over with me. I realized, of course, that I was being weighed. It should have been slightly embarrassing, for if I were found wanting on too many counts I should be deprived of a trip. On the other hand, if I were just too fascinating the gallant gentlemen might be loath to drown me. Anyone can see the meeting was a crisis.

I learned that the Fokker had been bought from Commander Byrd by the Honorable Mrs. Frederick Guest, of London, whose husband had been in the Air Ministry of Lloyd George and is prominently associated with aviation in Great Britain. Mrs. Guest, formerly Miss Amy Phipps of Pittsburgh, financed the expedition from first to last, and it was due entirely to her generosity and sportsmanship that opportunity to go was given me.

The transfer of ownership of the plane from Commander Byrd to Mrs. Guest had been kept secret. It had been her desire to hop off for the Atlantic crossing without attracting any advance attention. When subsequently, for personal reasons, Mrs. Guest herself abandoned the flight she was still eager to have the plans consummated, if possible, with an American woman on board.

A few days later I was told the flight actually would be made and that I could go—if I wished. Under the circumstances there was only one answer. I couldn't say no. For here was fate holding out the best in the way of flying ability in the person of Wilmer Stultz, pilot, aided by Lou Gordon as flight mechanic; and a beautiful ship admirably equipped for the test before it.

When I first saw *Friendship* she was jacked-up in the shadows of a hangar at East Boston. Mechanics and welders worked nearby on the struts for the pontoons that were shortly to replace the wheels. The ship's golden wings, with their spread of seventy-two feet, were strong and exquisitely fashioned. The red orange of the fuselage, though blending with the gold, was chosen not for artistry but for practical use. If we had come down orange could have been seen further than any other color.

The plane just then was being equipped, presumably for its use on Byrd's forthcoming Antarctic trip. Stultz and Gordon were supposed to be in Byrd's employ, and Commander Robert Elmer, U.S.N. retired, was directing technical activities.

Our purpose was to keep the plans secret. Once the world knew, we should be submerged in a deluge of curiosity making it impossible to continue the preparations in orderly fashion. Then, too, it would do no good to aviation to invite discussion of a project which some accident might delay. Actually the pontoon equipment on this type of plane was experimental, and no one definitely could tell in advance whether or not it would prove practicable. Another objection was the possibility of instigating a "race," which no one wanted. Mrs. Guest proposed that the *Friendship*, as she afterwards named the plane, should cross the Atlantic irrespective of the action of others. By our example we did not want to risk hurrying ill-prepared aspirants into the field with possible tragic results.

Only twice did I actually see the *Friendship* during all this time. I was pretty well known at the landing fields and obviously it might provoke comment if I seemed too interested in the plane. For this reason I had no chance to take part in any of the test flying. Actually the first time I was off the water in the *Friendship* was the Sunday morning when we finally got under way.

The preparation of a large plane for a long flight is a complex task. It is one that cannot—or at least should not—be rushed. Especially is that fact true where, as in the case of the *Friendship*, the equipment was of a somewhat experimental nature.

Throughout the operations Commander Byrd kept in close touch with what was being done, with Stultz and Gordon, and with Commander Elmer, who was overseeing the technical detail. Necessary instruments were installed and gradually tried out; while varying load tests, countless take-offs from the bay, and brief flights around Boston were made. The radio was tested and the inevitable last minute changes and adjustments arranged.

With the radio, we were particularly fortunate because Stultz is a skilful operator. It is unusual to find a man who is a great pilot, an instrument flyer, navigator, and a really good radio operator all in one.

Finally the ship itself was ready to go, and our problems focused on the weather. At this stage weather is an important factor in all plans of trans-oceanic flying.

Supplementing the meagre reports available from ships to the Weather Bureau, the *Friendship*'s backers arranged a service of their own. Special digests of the British reports were cabled to New York each morning, and meteorological data were radioed in from the ships at sea. All this information, supplementing that already at hand, was then coordinated and plotted out in the New York office of the United States Weather Bureau. There we came to feel that no flight could have a better friend than Dr. James H. Kimball, whose interest and unfailing helpfulness were indispensable.

The weather service for a flight such as ours must be largely planned and entirely underwritten by the backers of the flight itself. And, like so much else, it is an expensive undertaking.

Nearly three weeks dragged by in Boston. Sometimes Mr. and Mrs. Layman were there, hoping for an immediate take-off, sometimes Mrs. Putnam. Commander Elmer and Mr. Putnam were on hand constantly. Mrs. Guest's sons, Winston and Raymond, followed the preparations as closely as they dared without risking disclosure of the ownership.

It was during this period that I had the pleasure of seeing something of Commander and Mrs. Byrd, at their Brimmer Street home, just then bursting with the preparations for his Antarctic expedition—a place of tents and furs, specially devised instruments, concentrated foodstuffs, and all the rest of the paraphernalia which makes the practical, and sometimes the picturesque, background of a great expedition. There I met "Scotty" Allan, famous Alaskan dog driver, who was advising Byrd as to canine preparations.

The weather remained persistently unfavorable. When it was right in Boston, the mid-Atlantic was forbidding. I have a memory of long grey days which had a way of dampening our spirits against our best efforts to be cheerful. We tried to be casual by keeping occupied. On fair days my battered Kissel roadster, dubbed "Yellow Peril," was a means for sightseeing. On rainy days the top leaked too much for comfort, so we walked. We tried restaurants of all nationalities for variety and went, I think, to all the theatres.

One of the last plays we saw, I remember, was "The Good Hope," with the charming Eva LeGallienne. The story is a tragedy; all the hopeful characters drown while the most tragic one survives to carry out a cold lamb chop in the last act. A recurring line is "The fish are dearly paid for," and our crew adopted that as a heraldic motto, emblazoned under a goldfish rampant. I had the opportunity of thanking Miss LeGallienne for her cheering sendoff when I met her on returning to

New York. She helped Charles Winninger auction off one of the flags we carried on the flight, at a theatrical performance for the benefit of the Olympic team which was about to sail for Europe on the ship which had brought us back, the President Roosevelt. Anyway, that evening she got us on the stage before 17,280,891 people, so we have two grievances against her.

As I look back on the flight I think two questions have been asked me most frequently. First: Was I afraid? Secondly: What did I wear?

I'm sorry to be a disappointment in answering the first query. It would sound more exciting if I only could admit having been shockingly frightened. But I honestly wasn't. Of course I realized there was a measure of danger. Obviously I faced the possibility of not returning when first I considered going. Once faced and settled there really wasn't any good reason to refer to it again. After all, even when driving one admits tacitly there is danger, but one doesn't dwell on the result of losing the front wheels or having the rear end fall out on a mountain.

Perhaps the second question may be thought feminine, but I have had as many men as women appear interested.

Remember the early stages of automobiling? In those days an "auto" ride was a rare experience, made rarer by the clothes one wore. A linen duster, gauntlets and a veil were the requisites of touring in 1907.

Fashions in air clothing are emerging from the same sort of chrysalis stage. For routine short flights I

wear every-day clothes—what one would use for street wear
or sports. But obviously the *Friendship* flight was different. Compare it, perhaps, to a strenuous camping trip.
One couldn't tell what might happen. Serviceability was
the prime requirement. I had to wear breeks because of
the jump from the pontoon to the door and also because
of the necessity of slipping on and off the flying suit which
is worn outside one's other clothing.

In Boston I remember a solicitous friend wished
to give me a bag for extra clothing.

"There isn't going to be any," I explained.

That appeared to concern him somewhat—
certainly much more than it did me. There seems to be
a feeling that a woman preparing to drop in on England,
so to speak, ought to have something of a wardrobe.

However, I chose to take with me only what I had
on. The men on the *Friendship* took no "extras." Pounds—
even ounces—can count desperately. Obviously I should
not load up with unessentials if they didn't.

I'm told it's interesting to know exactly what the
outfit included. Just my old flying clothes, comfort-
ably, if not elegantly, battered and worn. High laced
boots, brown broadcloth breeks, white silk blouse with
a red necktie (rather antiquated!) and a com-
panionably ancient leather coat, rather long, with
plenty of pockets and a snug buttoning collar. A homely
brown sweater accompanied it. A light leather flying
helmet and goggles completed the picture, such as it
was. A single elegance was a brown and white silk scarf.

When it was cold I wore—as did the men—a heavy fur-lined flying suit which covers one completely from head to toe, shoes and all. Mine was lent to me by my friend Major Charles H. Woolley of Boston, who, by the way, had no idea when he lent it what it was to be used for. He suspected, I think, that I intended to do some high flying.

Toilet articles began with a toothbrush and ended with a comb. The only extras were some fresh hand-kerchiefs and a tube of cold cream. My "vanity case" was a small army knapsack.

Equipment was simple, too. Mr. Layman let me take his camera and Mrs. Layman her wrist watch. Field glasses, with plenty of use in the Arctic behind them, were lent me by G. P .P., and I was given a compact log book.

Besides toothbrushes—generic term—and food, our "baggage" was a book and a packet of messages which some of those associated with the enterprise asked to have carried across to friends on the other side.

The book—perhaps the only one to have crossed the Atlantic by air route—is Skyward, written by Commander Richard Evelyn Byrd. He sent it to Mrs. Guest. Commander Byrd, of course, had owned the *Friendship* and has outstandingly sponsored the wisdom of utilizing tri-motored ships equipped with pon-toons, for long-distance over-water flying. So it was appropriate that his book should be taken to the woman who bought his plane and made the trans-Atlantic flight possible.

This copy of his book which I delivered bears the following inscription: "I am sending you this copy of my first book by the first girl to cross the Atlantic Ocean by air—the very brave Miss Earhart. But for circumstances I well know that it would have been you who would have crossed first. I send you my heartiest congratulations and good wishes. I admire your determination and courage."

CHAPTER 6

OFF FOR NEWFOUNDLAND

TWICE, WHEN THE weather eastward seemed right, we tried to take off. And twice we failed because of too much fog or too little wind.

Three thirty!

Another day. Another start. Would it flatten out into failure like its predecessors?

Out of the hotel we trooped in the greyness of before-dawn. Another breakfast at an all-night eating place—Stultz and his wife, Gordon, his fiancée, Mrs. Layman, Lou and Mrs. Gower, Commander and Mrs. Elmer, George Palmer Putnam, "Jake" Coolidge, and a few others. An hour earlier the sandwiches had been made, the patient big thermos bottle again filled with coffee for the boys, the little one with cocoa for me.

We drove through deserted streets to T Wharf and at once boarded the tugboat Sadie Ross. The plane, as before, lay moored off the Jeffrey Yacht Club in East

Boston. Stultz, Gordon, Gower, and I climbed in. We said no "good-byes"—too many of them already, and too little going!

Slim uncovered the motors. Bill tinkered a bit with his radio and in the cockpit. Slim dropped down from the fuselage to the starboard pontoon, hopped over to the other, and cranked the port motor. Soon all three were turning over and *Friendship* taxied down the harbor, with the tug, carrying our friends, trailing us.

And then, suddenly, the adventure began—the dream became actuality.

We were off!

But let me tell the story here as I wrote it that very morning, in the little notebook that went with me across the Atlantic. Here is that record, exactly as it was set down (often none too legibly!) in my log book, penciled as we in the *Friendship* flew northeastward, with Boston behind and Newfoundland ahead:

* * *

Log Book:

7 o'clock, June 3. Slim has the controls and Bill is tuning in. He has been getting our position. I squat on the floor next the m.p. [motion picture] camera with my feet on a dunnage bag. There is one man's shoe in the passageway between

the gas tanks. It looks odd, but no one cares about its out-of-placeness.

We are flying at about 2,000 feet. There is a light haze and the ocean is smooth, with little color. From a height it looks quiet, almost like ice with flecks in it.

Boston is lost to view and has been for minutes. I tried to get a picture of the tugboats and harbor as we left, but just before starting the spring lock of the cabin door broke off, and I had to hold the door shut until Slim could get back to repair it. It was at first anchored to a gasoline can, but I saw the can being slowly pulled out, so anchored myself to it instead.

So, a few minutes after the take-off we nearly lost two of our crew. That would have been a jolly beginning! Actually Slim came within inches of falling out when the door suddenly slid open. And when I dived for that gasoline can, edging towards the opening door, I, too, had a narrow escape. However, a string tied through the leather thong in the door itself and fastened to a brace inside the cabin held it shut fairly securely.

* * *

Log Book:

The take-off was an eventful period. The wind was fair and the water slightly ruffled. When we started from the tug the sun was just coming over the rim of the harbor. A few dawn clouds hung about in the pink glow. The camera men and small group who came to see the departure were in a happy mood. For the third time they had assembled. Twice before the weather had prevented a getaway. The rehearsals had made all familiar with the process of arising at 3:30 and boarding a tug at 4:30 for a "fishing trip." Twice the thermos bottles had been filled and dumped and twice sandwiches had been replaced. This morning the whole thing was an old act. There were not so many present, as I had told the four friends of mine who knew of the flight, not to come. I didn't fancy another farewell and return a short while later. However, when we got out into the harbor, a small launch came chugging up and in it were my banished friends.

We were taxiing along toward open water and wind. A few craft were stirring, but Sunday morning does not bring out the usual activity. Before, in trying to get off we passed many small fishing dories and even had to avoid the New York boat which was just coming in.

This time all I could see was the silhouette of the various landmarks in the harbor. In the early morning light it was impossible to distinguish colors.

Bill headed the plane into the wind and gave her everything she had. We flew over the water, but the drag of the pontoons held us down. We tried again from a greater distance and still the water wouldn't let us go. Out went six five-gallon cans of gasoline—we had only eight—for another try.

Ordinarily a ship of this type is equipped with two wing tanks, which carry 95 gallons of gasoline. We had four. Many people don't realize, when they see a monoplane in the air, the thickness of the wings. From bottom to top the wing of *Friendship* measured about twenty-eight inches in some places; but after all this, in comparison with the great wing spread of seventy-two feet, gives an appearance of slightness. For a long cruise extra gasoline carrying capacity is needed, so *Friendship* was equipped with two special tanks, elliptical affairs, which bulged into the space just aft of the cockpit usually occupied by passengers.

There was room between these tanks to squeeze through. Fortunately the physical architecture of all three members of the *Friendship*'s crew was distinctly Gothic. But even at that the two boys had to turn sidewise to get through, while I, most Gothic of all, could contrive a straight-away entrance. It was between these two tanks that I spent many hours of the voyage, because into this space there wafted back some of the warmth from the heater in the cockpit. The after part of the cabin was unheated and often reached uncomfortably low temperatures.

In addition to the gas carried in the wing and these supplementary tanks, we had on board a limited amount in five-gallon tins. This was not only a supplementary supply, but was carried in this form for quick dumping in case of emergency. It was advantageous, too, to have the weight distributed well astern. In taking off, all of us, except Bill, crowded as far aft as we could.

* * *

Log Book:
  Mr. Gower came back into the hold in order to force the nose up as far as possible. To no avail.

* * *

Lou Gower is an expert pilot, with much big-ship experience, who had been retained as a sort of understudy for Stultz in case of sickness or accident. It was hoped he could go as far as Trepassey, there to share the work of the two men who actually would carry through on the Atlantic flight.

* * *

Log Book:

As Bill turned the ship's nose around, Gower began pulling his flying suit from the bag. His shoes and a small personal package were all he had in addition. Slim called for a boat from the tug and G. bade us adieu very quietly. I didn't want him to go, but of course realized he was the only one to leave and a sacrifice of something was necessary to be able to get off. He is a dependable person, a true sport who appreciates a situation very quickly, and an excellent pilot. As soon as the little boat came from the tug with R. E. and G. P. P. aboard, Gower left us.

For the first time then I felt the *Friendship* really lighten on the water and knew the difference of a few pounds had made her a bird.

67 seconds to get off. We bank, swoop down and with gathering speed zoom over the tug. I hope the cameras [those on the

tug] registered, for the ship looks beautiful in flight.

* * *

All that was written in the first part of the journey after
leaving Boston. It was less than an hour out when the
next entry in the diary is recorded.

* * *

Log Book:

I can see fifteen little fishing vessels.
Probably they can't see each other.

96 miles out (1 hour). 7:30. 2500 ft. Bill
shows me on the map that we are near Cash's
Ledge. We cannot see anything (if there is
anything to see), as the haze makes visibility
poor. The sun is blinding in the cockpit
and will be, for a couple of hours. Bill is
crouching by the hatchway, taking sights.

* * *

The drift indicator was on the floor by the hatchway
which had to be opened each time speed and drift
calculations were made.

* * *

Log Book:

Hooray! Nova Scotia at 8:55. Fear Island. We are flying at 2000. I can look down and see many white gulls flying over the green land. A few houses are clustered together, and a dory is pulled up on the shore. There is a rocky ledge around the islands which makes a ruffle. They look very flat and the trees are foreshortened.

We are making good time with the wind's help.

I have in my ears some little rubber ear stops which Mrs. Byrd sent. She said Commander B. had used them in his trans-Atlantic flight, and was the only one who could hear when the plane reached the other side. I am eager to see whether they work, as both the men are without them.

Pubnico Harbor is below. Bill figures 114 m.p.h. since we left Boston. What a jagged coast. There are few roads. Many little houses nestle in the woods seemingly out of communication with anything for miles.

One can see deeply into the water and mark shoals and currents. What an easy way to see what are bugaboos for surface craft.

The haze is not so marked now and the

wind is rougher. This ship flies smoothly, but I know a smaller one would be tossed about.

The color of the sand about the edges of the water differs; some is white, some rusty. I cannot see any breakers, except far out—the sea is calm with sparking ripples.

Our shadow skims over the treetops. The people whom I cannot see are probably used to the sight and sound of strange planes.

* * *

During the last two years this remote country has had many visitors from the air. These people, I think, have come to feel a real intimacy with the flyers. There have been Lindbergh and Byrd, de Pinedo, Mrs. Grayson, possibly Old Glory, and in the old days, the N. C. 4's, disregarding the incidental flights which doubtless have winged over this territory.

* * *

Log Book:

What makes people live on little jets of land like this one?

White, white sand and curving wrinkled water, windswept and barren.

I have changed my seat to a gas can, one of the two saved this morning.

A green mottled shore line comes into view. We are running into clouds and haze again. The former are scudding fast, but we outdistance them.

The motors are humming sweetly.

* * *

Continued. I have dozed off and awake to find us flying at 2000 above a sea of fog. The wind is rough and Bill is shutting off the motors. I suppose we shall go down through it to see where we are. As far as one can see there are swirls of white cloud.

Oh, the weather! The sun is shining above here, but the haze is becoming greater. We are now about 500 feet over the water. Land is to our left.

Since I wrote the last we have circled the harbor of Halifax twice and slipped to a landing. Bill went 30 miles beyond and found fog to the treetops, so came back to the clearing here.

The natives are swarming to the shore and several dories are coming out.

Bill and Slim are going over to the land to get reports with the hope we can go on later. I am to stay aboard now, as we all are, later, if there is chance of continuing.

The mournful sound of the fog horn disturbs my peace and hope. I hardly think we could take off here even without fog, as there is no wind at all. Well, anyway, I'd rather visit Halifax this way than any other I can think of.

An orange, carefully provided by G. P. P., tastes good. 'Tis my first food.

Bill and Slim have returned with news of rain and clouds ahead.

A light wind is springing up which may help the situation.

We are half-way to Trepassey. The coastline will help us in navigating for a while unless the fog cuts off the view.

Bill says he'll try to make T., so Slim is cranking up. A broken primer is found, but we start without soldering it, as time is precious. We have already lost an hour by change of time.

The fog and clouds look pretty bad. The Flight Sergeant at Halifax says we may return, and we agree. Bill says the Newfoundland coast is bad enough, but in a fog won't be tried.

We are flying blind on the right side, but can see a little on the left. Probably rain ahead.

I tried to take a m. p. of our leaving

Halifax. I had to take it through the glass, and don't imagine it will be worth much.

Time of leaving H. about 2:30.

Slim comes back to pump gas into the right tank from the small cans.

We are turning back. The fog spreads out ahead of us like a great fuzz. Into the clear again. What luck to have the fog block us!

Bill slips her into Halifax for a perfect landing just behind a Canadian Fairchild pontoon job. The Flight Sergeant comes over and helps to anchor her. After consultation we invite him in and put the situation of my retiring disposition before him.

* * *

When we were forced down in Halifax our difficulties of maintaining secrecy increased. Publicity, we feared, was probably unescapable. But at all events, escape seemed worth an effort. And especially, so far as possible, we thought it wise to conceal the presence of a woman on the *Friendship*. The Sergeant had the surprise of his life when he came aboard the plane to look over the equipment and found me part of it.

* * *

Log Book:

He thinks a government official will
take me in while the boys go to a hotel.
Consequently I stay on the plane while the
others go back to find out. They'll pick
me up later.

In the meantime a ham sandwich is
food. I don't dare take pictures lest the
people see I am present.

The plane rides at her moorings and
the waves of passing launches knock the
pontoons with hammer blows. Water is
very hard.

At last the gang comes for me. It is
decided to go to a small hotel in Dartmouth.
It is Sunday, and Orchard Day, besides
being the King's birthday. Consequently,
no one much is at home. We have difficulty
finding the proprietor of the hotel even.
He has no rooms in the main building
and we are shown to the Annex. It is very
informal. The key hangs behind the door
for all who know where to find it. A strange
billiard table rests in the main hall. Our
rooms are on the third floor.

This country would be grand for
camping. Real solitude with lovely little
lakes and bays. The pine trees don't look
attractive as landing fields, but do for

EARHART IN THE DOORWAY OF THE *FRIENDSHIP*

outings. Slim says in this connection that he was glad of pontoons for the first time, as he looked over the landscape.

12 P.M. Two reporters and camera men are in the next room trying to persuade Stultz and G. to dress and have a flashlight picture taken. I am displeased with their thoughtlessness in keeping the men (Bill and Slim) awake. I don't know whether the newspaper men know I am here so I am not shouting my sentiments.

It is now 9:45. We are out of Halifax about 15 minutes. The take-off took one minute in a perfectly calm sea. We loaded 100 gals. of gas after we had waited since about 7 A.M. until 9 for its arrival. Any other day in the year, I suppose, would have been better to get it. I wandered around and looked over the station, stopping a few minutes in what I was told was Commander Byrd's home when he was in charge of the station during the war. Major Harrup is there now and while the station is not active just now, is going to be soon, with several seaplanes assigned to it.

We had many encounters with newspaper men this morning. We were called at 5:30, and the hotel served us a little after six—unusual service for a holiday. Slim is feeling ill still, but managed to eat something. We had two pictures taken before breakfast; interviews at, and pictures and interviews afterward. When we arrived at the station we met more camera men and reporters.

We went over to the plane in the tug which carried the gas. I chatted with the men who handled it and was assured that rubbing gas and oil on one's hair made it grow and was good for it every day. We spilled some fuel on the water and I thought of the accident to De Pinedo's ship caused by throwing a cigarette on the water afterward.

The air is exceedingly rough today. We are flying at 2000. The land which was covered with fog yesterday is sparklingly clear today. The sea is beautifully blue and there are a few light clouds.

We have a sheaf of Halifax newspapers with strange assertions about us all. They will make strange reading matter if we ever have opportunity to re-read them.

Bill is trying to get some one to answer his signals. He can hear others and apparently can send. The radio man at Halifax said he'd listen and answer.

We are flying along the coast. The water appears shallow, as I can see the bottom in many places. A flock of birds rise from the water at our shadow. They resemble in movement and shape the spreading out of the little stars in a sky-rocket.

The inhabitants who come to look at us wear red shirts or skirts. Red seems to be a favorite rural color. Cows and horses don't like us.

What cruel rocks these ledges are. Sharp and narrow, they look like sharks.

I move to sit on a gas can by the window. What a comfortable passenger plane this would be with the gas tanks removed and windows made in the sides.

There is a small steamer to the right. I wonder if she knows who we are. I wonder if we know.

* * *

There is more sea than land now and we fly at 1800.

In a way, I am glad of the stop at Halifax, for I always think it better for a motor to run gradually to long grinds.

We can see a haze. Reports last night said 200 miles of fog. I hope all 200 miles of it have gone away. (Temperature outside: 52°. Inside: 58°.)

Bill shows me where we are. 11:55 and the plane is off Cape Canso. He is trying radio again and has hooked up the other set.

The wind is steadier over the sea.

Slim comes back for a sandwich. We seem to have endless ham sandwiches. Coffee and cocoa will be taken on at Trepassey and a few fresh things.

* * *

This plethora of ham sandwiches, it developed, was our own fault. We simply didn't explore far enough. Three generous lunches had been prepared for us by the Copley Plaza Hotel, arranged for a "fishing trip." The tactical error was putting all the ham sandwiches on the top layer. We never got beyond them. Later, to our chagrin, we discovered that below there were similar layers of delicious chicken and tongue sandwiches, hard boiled eggs and much beside. We never had the courage to determine exactly what else there might have been.

The gastronomic adventures of trans-oceanic flying really deserve a record of their own. Our own highlights were varied. Ham sandwiches seemed to predominate en route. At Trepassey it was canned rabbit, in London the desserts were strawberries, and home again in America chicken appeared invariably on all state occasions.

* * *

Log Book:

Bill has been flying. G. now has controls. The sea looks like the back of an elephant, the same kind of wrinkles.

Nothing but blue sea. A low rim of fog far to the right.

Hooray! Bill has picked up a station. 12:15. He is taking something.

We are flying at 3200 ft. Temperature down to 53° inside.

The fog bank is nearer and looks pretty thick. It shadows the water. We are nosing down and the air is rougher. The motors are racing, and the a.s.i. [air speed indicator] registers 100 m.p.h. It has been about 86.

12:50. Newfoundland sighted to the left. More fog to the rt. than in direction we wish. I notice the motors synchronize every five seconds at the speed they are running.

Change of time 2:00 P.M. Bill says we are making in actual speed 115 m.p.h.

2:20. A steamer sighted to the left. We are too far from it for me to take a picture. Anyway we are running with considerable haze.

2:35. We have left the sun behind and are just under a bank of clouds. Alt. 3000.

St. Mary's Bay in sight. 2:50. Visibility better. Clear toward sea. The fog hangs in white curly masses over the land.

We are near Trepassey. What is in store for us?

* * *

We had expected a pretty routine landing and so I crawled into the cockpit to take pictures of the reception committee. But as a matter of fact *Friendship*'s arrival resembled a rodeo. At once a dozen small boats began to circle madly about us, the local motto seeming to be that the early boat catches the plane. It happened that we had arranged for a mooring of our own to which we wished to be directed. But each local optimist felt that if he contrived to get us in tow first he could take the prize to his own mooring and reap appropriate reward.

Poised in the bows of the launches each maritime cowboy whirled aloft a coil of rope, attempting to cast it at us. Slim, out on the pontoon, was doing his best to keep clear and yelled frantically to ward them off. The noise of the idling motors, augmented by the racket of the small boats, made hearing difficult. I was convulsed with laughter. In the cockpit, Bill, I fear, was talking to God about it. What concerned him most was the risk of ropes becoming entangled in the propellers, and especially the danger to the visitors themselves in getting too close to whirling props. At the height of the excitement enthusiasm completely overcame one would-be welcomer. He hurled his rope and landed a bull's eye on Slim, nearly knocking him into the water. Fortunately I couldn't hear what Slim said; at best his enthusiasm for marine affairs was never notable.

The tempo of the maritime merry-go-round was extraordinary. Truly, I've never had a more entertaining half hour.

Finally we contrived to get the thought across that the most we wanted was to be guided to our own mooring, which we could reach under our own power. Andy Fulgoni, Paramount camera man, finally caught the idea and circling around in his own launch contrived to clear the way for us. In due course, Bill sailed to the mooring and made fast.

CHAPTER 7

AT TREPASSEY

LOG BOOK:

June 5,—2:45. There is a howling gale outside. The wind has blown steadily since we arrived and is getting worse now. Bill says it would be grand if we were in the air, but we can't take off against the hill across the bay. We'd have to turn and turning would mean a slide into the water, with a heavily loaded plane and side wind.

Slim is aboard now repairing a crack in oil tank with cement and adhesive tape. It was thought first that the case would have to be taken off—an impossible job in the wind.

Everything is being done for a possible departure. The radio was cutting out yesterday but today Bill says he found the trouble in a loose connection.

We are lodged in one of the mansions of the town.

It is difficult to raise anything here but "badadoes," "tornips" and cabbage. Each family has a garden, a few sheep and usually a cow.

The stove here is a three-decker, with the oven on top. Heavy iron kettles and pots are used for cooking. Tea and coffee only are known. Houses are clean and fences whitewashed.

I could enjoy myself were it not for anxiety about a take-off today, and the disgusting news of publicity. Every few minutes a telegraph operator patters over and hands me a telegram from some one. Some are lovely, and others disturb me greatly. The latest says B. papers carry a story I went to recoup fallen fortunes of family.

A photographer is on the way. The train has just pulled in—it comes twice a week, and the town watches to see who gets off.

(Continued after tea.) The boys have come. All are cheerful. One by one the natives drop in to see us.

I was welcomed at the landing as the first woman to come to Newfoundland.

I didn't get the point. Perhaps the agent mean flyin'. I dunno. I said I was honored. He said Nfld. was. La de da.

School had been let out early and I have a vision of many white pinafores and aprons on the dock. As soon as we stepped ashore we were given three cheers and the (aforementioned) government agent rushed up. Also the telegraph operator with three telegrams for me. We were led to a dinner of chicken and dandelions and "badadoes."

Mrs. Deveraux (at the home of whom we are lodged) was quite overcome, and felt me to be sure I was present in the flesh.

We may not get off tomorrow as the wind is as violent as ever; which means the expected storm is coming nearer.

The wind held the key to our problems. For three days it blew briskly from the northwest. This was ideal for the flight itself, but far from ideal locally, as it stirred up such sea it was impossible to load the gasoline with safety. What's more, Bill feared that the heavy weight of the load left on board the *Friendship* might seriously injure her as she was buffeted about in the rough water.

The necessity of landing at all at Trepassey was a

tragedy for us, the extent of which became apparent during the fortnight of delay which followed. Had we been able to carry enough gas from Halifax we certainly would have kept on eastward as the flying conditions on the day of our arrival appeared ideal. But once in Trepassey we were trapped.

* * *

Log Book:

(Next morning.) The wind is changing though still stormy. The additional gas is being put aboard and Bill, after looking over the situation, is snoozing. The wind is veering back and forth, now from S. now from N.? The old-timers say a S.W. wind is due. We hope so!!!!!

After supper, June 6. Bill has just been flying the kite and trying out the emergency radio. Andy Fulgoni, Claud Frazer and I went into the doctor's and heard his signals very plainly. He was trying to reach Cape Race. Just now the gang has gone to W.U., and I haven't heard whether they were successful.

We have spent one indolent day. After the excitement of the morning, when the wind seemed to be shifting permanently, all of us had a sleep. Bill chopped a little wood. Slim and I played "rummy." I read one of the six books here, "The Story of the Titanic Disaster." We have read telegrams and scanned maps and weather reports. I took a walk with Andy and Claud Frazer.

For supper we had canned rabbit. Bill's comment when he first tasted it was: "Here's something they caught last year—something that couldn't get away."

We had fish today for the first time— canned last year in Newfoundland. Slim hates fish, and had been told that was all there was to eat. Also that even eggs would taste of fish because hens were fed on fish. He has been eating chocolates by the package and seems to thrive.

* * *

Slim hails from Texas. Geographically and tempera- mentally he is no sailor. Even the word "pontoon" made him stutter a bit, and neither salt water nor its prod- ucts held any joy for him. Consequently he had been plentifully stuffed with stories of what life meant in a fishing village by the sea. To make matters worse he had had a severe attack of ptomaine poisoning from eat- ing clams in Boston just before we started. The only escape led to the little local store and its limited supply of candy. Before we left we had completely absorbed its entire stock.

* * *

Log Book:

Bill has just come in, with weather reports. He has wired Byrd for confirmation of plans and advice. If the wind holds as now (from north) we can get away. The old codgers talking here, told me the wind calms down about 4 A.M. so I suggested we get out of this trap and into the next harbor. The change in the wind may make this unnecessary. The boys have retired in the hope the wind stays as is, or moves north.

Funny spelling in the paper from St. John's. "D'oyleys" meaning little paper mats. The language is peculiar. There are too many "r's." And often an "oi" sound where one doesn't belong. "Poilet" for pilot.

I investigated hooked rugs today. Mrs. D. has them all over the house; some made from cotton washed ashore twenty years ago from a wreck. By the way, much of the silver and some furniture is from wrecks which ground on this "Graveyard of the Atlantic."

* * *

The cruelty of country and climate is surely a contrast to the kind hearts of the people of Newfoundland. They were untiringly good to us.

* * *

Log Book:

June 7, 1928.

After an early rise to get the ship ready, the wind calmed, and we waited for it to freshen and also for weather reports. After getting favorable ones we thought about noon we would be able to get off, as the wind changed and water grew rough.

In vain we tried three times and had to give up. Slim had cemented a pontoon which had sprung a leak and is now soldering the cracked oil tank which the cement and adhesive tape didn't repair.

Just now Bill is playing on a strange instrument with Andy. They are trying to learn it from directions given. The fence is lined with listeners who are starved for music. The only music here is two "Gramophones"—this instrument, a "guitar harp"—and a piano. The fence is lined with men as soon as any music is started. Though the people crave it, they don't try to have any. How different from the expressive South! Here emotions are as unexpressed as nature is barren.

Friday. Is it possible we have been here so long? I didn't get up very early ce matin as I depended upon being waked. The thing which did get me up was the strain of "Jingle Bells" played by Wilmer Stultz on the strange instrument described before. Just now Slim is asleep.

Bill and Andy and Frazer out in a dory with a sail. Bill has my leather coat as neither of the boys brought anything but ordinary coats.

They played at tying knots all the morning, and Slim and I had "rummy" games. I have been having a terrific run of luck—winning every game nearly, at a cent a point. We played until after ten last night—very late hour for us.

The men are simply great under the strain. Our hopes are high today as the barometer is rising and everything points to favorable weather soon.

I went out in a launch yesterday and was run on the rocks. The leak made was so bad that the boat had to be beached this morning for repairs. The water is shallow along the shore, and, as I have said before, the rocks are cruel.

The men from here go fishing next week and will be gone five weeks. They are preparing for their voyages now. I should think they'd get out of the habit of working. I am sure they would if living didn't have to be scratched for so hard.

Compared with Tyler St. the children here seem very quiet. I think they are unusually so anyway. I just heard two make some noise and it sounded very strange. Of course, they are shy, too.

For two years I have been associated with Denison House, Boston's old settlement center on Tyler Street, where the children are anything but quiet. There they are mostly Chinese and Syrians. All city children somehow seem noisy. Perhaps that is because of their cramped surroundings. And especially, of course, the urban child is boldly independent, while the children of remote communities have so little contact with the outer world that they are self-conscious with strangers.

* * *

Log Book:

June 9, 1928.

The evening of the day is here. The boys and I played "rummy" all the morning and I lost for a change. At luncheon we had lamb stew. Apparently no one knows about cooking lamb except by boiling. I should love to have a chop. At supper we had fresh salmon. It was delicious. Slim and I sat and talked over the meal while Bill went to W.U. The boys had been out fishing in the afternoon. They started to explore a cave but found the water too rough. There are two good caves here which have never been explored. How I'd like to explore them. There might be buried treasure—in fact, there have been several attempts to dig up some at the other end of the bay. I don't know who the "buriers" are supposed to be.

Mr. Deveraux has just come in and suggested we go eeling. I have just returned from a walk and the boys from Fulgoni's. Eeling is off. The gang is going down on a gasoline rail car for a ride. They have wired the Supt. for permission to use it and are off to Biscay Bay. They wear their flying suits, as the wind is really cold.

Our telegrams decreased today. I

had time to wash my hair. I wish I had
manicuring facilities and a bath tub.

June 10.

The indefatigable Bill insisted on
going eeling or trouting or exploring.
Slim refused to get up and slept until
five. Bill dragged the other two, and two
natives, with him to the other end of the
bay. They constructed an eel trap before
they left but took poles too. At six they
returned with some beautiful speckled
trout, nearly all caught by B. S. He hiked
back into the woods to a stream while
the others sat and caught one sea trout
from the boat.

Fog has come in thick and woolly
and rain is now accompanying. The
weather reports sound favorable but there
is no chance of our getting out of this fog
I fear. Job had nothing on us. We are just
managing to keep from suicide.

June 11.

The fog has cleared and I think a
wind is coming. Bill has a hunch we move
soon. I hope he is right. We have not yet
received G. P.'s report.

10:35 P.M. I have never been so
faithful to a diary. No luck today. We
could have got off here but the Atlantic

wasn't inviting. Reports today say mayhap tomorrow noon will be propitious.

The gang went to see the old spiked cannon on the hill at the mouth of the bay. They are overgrown and are at least 200 yrs. old. They bear G.R. on them. We all came home and tried to work puzzles the whole evening.

Andy has a passion for stuffing the town gossip here, so slipped out to tell him the usual string of stories for the day. This morning he had him (the t.g.) up at five for the take-off which he promised rain or shine.

Oh, if only we can get away soon. It is hard indeed to remain sans books, sans contact with one's interests and withal on a terrific strain.

The wind is chill tonight and even with a flannel nightgown I know I shall shiver.

* * *

The flannel nightgown referred to was borrowed and I began to feel that even its sturdy fabric would be worn out before we ever got away from Trepassey—although I didn't know about the wearing qualities of flannel gowns, never having had one before. Incidentally its warmth was supplemented by the down beds upon which we slept and into which we sank luxuriously.

I have said my outfit consisted of a toothbrush and two handkerchiefs when we shoved off from Boston. The toothbrush was holding out, which is more than I can say for some of the rest of my personal equipment.

After a week of waiting, a telegram came from G. P. P. in New York.

"Suggest you turn in and have your laundering done."

To which I dispatched this reply:

G.P. PUTNAM

NEW YORK

THANKS FATHERLY TELEGRAM   NO WASHING NECESSARY SOCKS UNDERWEAR WORN OUT SHIRT LOST TO SLIM AT RUMMY CHEERIO

A E

9IOPM

It is a long time since I have bought hose at 35c a pair. That was top-price in Trepassey. A khaki shirt was another purchase. With a safety pin taking a tuck in the back of the collar, it fitted reasonably well.

Bill and I wore the same size shirt. An echo of its tailoring came later when Mrs. Stultz confessed to me that on first seeing Bill's Trepassey purchase she had asked him what it was.

* * *

Log Book:

>June 12.
>
>This has been the worst day.
>
>We tried for four hours to get away in a wind we had been praying for. The most unexpected and disappointing circumstance ruined the take-off. The receding tide made the sea so heavy that the spray was thrown so high that it drowned the outboard motors. As we gathered speed, the motors would cut and we'd lose the precious pull necessary.
>
>The ship seemed so loggy that Bill felt there must be water in the pontoons. So Slim stayed on the job and opened every hatch to see. He found only about a gallon and swears he'll never open another one.
>
>We unloaded every ounce of stuff from the plane—camera, my coat, bags, cushions, etc.
>
>She would have gone but for the motors. There was salt water above the prop. hubs.
>
>I received some letters today and Andy brought over some "day after the take-off" papers in Boston. I couldn't

read them under the circumstances of
this day. We were all too disappointed to
talk. The boys are in bed and I am going
soon. We rise at six.

Wednesday Evening.

The days grow worse. I think each
time we have reached the low, but find
we haven't.

Vainly we tried to rise today with
our load.

Today Bill and Slim tried to take her
off after she had been "degassed" by 300
lbs. The left motor cut and they could-
n't get her off light. While working with
it they set some yokel to watch the tide,
but he forgot, and it ran out leaving
them on a sandy ledge. They got the
motor repaired and will have to go out at
midnight to float her down to the buoy.
We may try for the Azores tomorrow, if
possible at dawn.

I went to the Catholic School for
maps but found nothing helpful but a
huge globe. I promised to write the sis-
ters if we hit land anywhere. I am going
to bed as I can't help and none of us are
sleeping much any more and we need all
we can get. We are on the ragged edge.

Bill is getting ship reports at midnight

tonight and will make his own weather
map from them.

* * *

The next log book entry emphasizes our isolation.
The only newspapers we'd seen had been a stray batch
from Boston, describing the take-off. By then that
seemed in the dark ages. So far as we knew we were com-
fortably forgotten by the world. Echoes only came to
us in personal messages, and at that time it was impossible to realize that any general interest remained.

* * *

Log Book:

Apparently from the telegrams to
me today our troubles are painted heavily for they all say—"stick to it," "we're
for you," etc. One inventor has written
he will install his invention gratuitously
and guarantee we can get off with maximum load. Our efficiency will be
increased 35% etc. It will take only a
month to get the apparatus here, and
twelve hours to install. We all wish we had
a dozen with us.

I saw an interesting stunt. There are
wells here and all water has to be carried

to the houses. A little girl—a really little girl—put two buckets of H_2O on a stick and then separated the buckets by a barrel hoop and stepped inside. Thus she could carry the two without having them hit her legs.

The evening of the 15th day. We have had a musical evening again tonight. The old harp was bro't forth and Bill and Andy played. It is very funny to see two able-bodied men picking out "Jingle Bells." Two are required for the feat and I am terribly amused. Bill has a good deal of music in him and knows some Spanish stuff of which I am very fond.

Today has been happier as a whole. We all appeared this morning vowing to change clothes and clean up. I bought a 90c green checked Mother Hubbard, the best in stock and a pair of tan hose. With borrowed shoes, skirt and slip, I pitched in and washed everything else. Bill borrowed trousers, and had his suit cleaned and pressed and his shirts laundered. He purchased a new tie as the one he had was fast "going to the devil" and some Trepassey socks. Slim also is spic and span. All we need are baths, manicures and haircuts—none of which are obtainable here.

∗ ∗ ∗

In those last days at Trepassey, one bit of news that did filter in from the outside world cheered us mightily. That was word of the successful flight of the Southern Cross from San Francisco across the Pacific. She was a tri-motor Fokker, engined with Wright Whirlwind motors, practically identical with the *Friendship* except that she was not equipped with pontoons.

They made it; so could we. Their accomplishment was a challenge.

CHAPTER 8

ACROSS

✳

LOG BOOK:

> Sunday—At the present time we have been out an hour. Land has gone in the haze and we are almost into the fog bank which hangs always off the coast of Newfoundland. We have 1500 ft. and both boys are in the cockpit. Me, I am holding down a pile of flying suits, as we left every ounce we could spare at Trepassey and the three cushions were among the things discarded.

> We made three tries before we got off and went up from a heavy sea with one motor so wet it has just come in full recently. We had to throw out all our canned gas. We have only 700 gals. with us now.

✳ ✳ ✳

"LADY LUCK" AND "LADY LINDY" IN A CARTOON FROM THE
NEW YORK *WORLD*

That was the first entry in the log book following the actual take-off from Trepassey. We left the harbor about 11:15 in the morning, having waited until then for final weather reports. The villagers had seen us "start" so often they had lost faith, so there were only a few on shore to see the *Friendship* take the air.

I had left a telegram to be sent half an hour after we had gone.

"Violet. Cheerio.

A. E."

That was the message. The code word "Violet" meant "We are just hopping off." That was our official good-bye to America.

* * *

Log Book:

A motion picture camera and the boys' thermos bottle left. We have only the small thermos filled with coffee for the boys. I shan't drink anything probably unless we come down.

* * *

By the way, our rations might be considered eccentric. About half of the five gallons of mineral water put on at Boston remained. There were three elephantine egg sandwiches. (Trepassey bread is home-made in round loaves.) Eight or nine oranges survived from the original supply. A couple of tins of Drake's oatmeal cookies were luxury. For emergency ration, we had a few tins of pemmican, a bottle of Horlick's Malted Milk tablets, and some Hershey's chocolate. And that, I think, completed the larder.

* * *

Log Book:

This ship takes off better in a fairly smooth sea, it seems. I have learned a lot and designers of pontoons have something to learn too.

We are skimming the fluffy top of the fog now, having wobbled through to 2500 feet. Bill is at the controls until we get out of it. He thinks we shall pass through alternate storm areas and clears the whole distance. Wisps of cloud flit past the windows of the cabin. Sometimes the fog obscures everything.

We are climbing fast to crawl over now. Almost 3000 ft.!

There is very blue sky above and when last I saw H_2O it was also brilliant.

As we left Newfoundland we flew about 1000 ft. over the land. I watch the shapes of the many lakes, large and small, which cover the terrain. Two are gigantic footprints; another a buffalo—another a prehistoric animal.

is this a pleseosaurus?

There were many "things" depicted
with lumpy paws and flat head and the
usual accumulation of abnormalities
belonging to the genus Thing. 3300 ft.
Over an extensive cushion of fleecy fog.
Bill has been at radio and writes CEV to
me. I grab call book and find SS.
Elmworth is calling.

Soon Cape Race asks how things are
going. We are at 5000 now getting out
of fog, but into a storm. A flurry of snow
just passed below. I can see clear weather
to right, but not ahead. Temperature
back here 42 degrees. I am not cold, as
I got used to cold in Trepassey.

Speaking of Fog again, I know
Dunsany would like to see the world above
the earth. Irish fogs have been described
in detail, and their bilious effect, and
their fairies and their little people. But no
one has written of a bird's-eye view of
one from an imaginative eye.

I may not be cold, but my coat will
make me more comfortable.

4000 ft. More than three tons of us
hurtling through the air. We are in the
storm now. 3 tons is shaken considerably.

✶ ✶ ✶

People are so likely to think of planes as frail craft that I draw attention to this entry. *Friendship* weighs 6000 pounds empty, and on the flight she carried about her own weight again.

✳ ✳ ✳

Log Book:

Bill is nosing her down, all motors wide.

We are bucking a head wind and rain. Heaviest storm I have ever been in, in the air, and had to go through. The sea below looks fairly placid, but of course the surface appears flat from 3000.

✳ ✳ ✳

A surprising element of flying, at first, is the flatness of the earth's contours as seen from above—even sizeable hills dwarf. This tendency gives one a feeling of security and a comfortable belief that a safe landing can be made almost anywhere.

"The higher the safer" is a good adage. The air itself isn't dangerous, as I have said before. The greater the altitude, the larger the pilot's choice in picking and being able to reach a landing field in an emergency.

Don't ask a pilot to stay close to the ground, unless he is flying over geographical billiard tables.

* * *

Log Book:

 I see some clear sea ahead and the air is getting bumpy, as one would expect between areas of cloud and sun. Slim comes back to say snow is in the air. I know it.

 I have just come back from sitting up front. Slim at the controls with Bill advising him. Bill has homing pigeon sense of direction....He tells Slim to keep at 106.

 We have been out of snow a long while now and the sun is shining and the water blue as far as one can see. There are some clouds ahead—what, I don't know. They look high and white.

* * *

Those clouds ahead continued from there on. Not again on the flight did we see the ocean. Skippy was right— it was no sea voyage.

* * *

Log Book:

 140 m.p.h. now. Wonderful time. Temp. 52. The heater from cockpit warms the cabin too.

Bill says radio is cuckoo. He is calling now.

There is so much to write. I wonder whether ol' diary will hold out.

I see clouds coming. They lie on the horizon like a long shore line.

I have just uncurled from lying on Major Woolley's suit for half an hour. I came off this morn with such a headache that I could hardly see. I thought if I put it to sleep it might get lost in the billows of fog we are flying over.

There is nothing to see but churned mist, very white in the afternoon sun. I can't see an end to it. 3600 ft. temp. 52, 45 degrees outside. I have et a orange, one of the originals. At T. our infrequent oranges came from Spain, under-nourished little bloods.

* * *

Very "original" those oranges, almost historic! They were purchased in Boston in the dark ages of the *Friendship*'s take-offs. In the three unsuccessful efforts during that fortnight of disappointments, they went out to the ship with us each morning and came back again to the hotel. But sturdy oranges they proved to be, and nearly a month later were still in good

form when they finally found a place on our mid-
Atlantic menu.

On the trans-Atlantic flight three oranges, appropriately from California, comprised my full bill-of-fare
with the exception of probably a dozen malted milk
tablets. The sandwiches and the coffee I left to the boys.
Somehow I wasn't hungry and, curiously, at the end of
the trip there still wasn't any particular desire for food.

* * *

Log Book:

    4:15. Bill has just opened the motor
to climb over this fog. We are 3800
and climbing.

    Creatures of fog rear their heads
above the surroundings. And what a wallop we get as we go through them.

    Bill has just picked up XHY British
Ship Rexmore, which gives us bearing.
48 no. 39 west 20:45 GMT. The fog is
growing patchy and great holes of ocean
can be seen. XHY will inform NY of
our position.

    As I look out of the window I see a true
rainbow—I mean the famous circle. It is of
course moving at our speed and is on our
right, sun being to port a trifle. I have
heard of color circles in Hawaii.

The sun is sinking behind a limitless sea of fog and we have a bright rainbow, a fainter ring and, if I am not seeing things, a third suggestion on the edge. The middle is predominately yellow with a round grey shadow in the center. Is it caused from us or our props?

* * *

This is not an unknown phenomenon. Sub-sequently I learned the rainbows were caused by our propellers.

* * *

Log Book:

I do believe we are getting out of the fog. Marvellous shapes in white stand out, some trailing shimmering veils. The clouds look like icebergs in the distance. It seemed almost impossible to believe that one couldn't bounce forever on the packed fog we are leaving. The highest peaks of the fog mountains, (oh, we didn't get out) are tinted pink, with the setting sun. The hollows are grey and shadowy. Bill just got the time. O. K. sez he. 10:20 London time my watch. Pemmican is being passed or just has been. What stuff!

The pink vastness reminds me of the Mojave Desert. Also: J'ai miré dans ma prunel Petite minute éblouie La grande lumière éternele. (Bill gets position. We are out 1096 miles at 10:30 London time,)—and having done so he is content to die. I wish I had that poem here.

One of the greatest sights is the sun splashing to oblivion behind the fog, but showing pink glows through apertures in the fog. I wish the sun would linger longer. We shall soon be grey-sheathed. We are sinking in the fog.
4000 ft.

The light of the exhausts is beginning to show as pink as the last glow of the sky. Endless foggies. The view is too vast and lovely for words. I think I am happy—sad admission of scant intellectual equipment.

I am getting housemaid's knee kneeling here at the table gulping beauty.

✱ ✱ ✱

I was kneeling beside the chart table, which was in front of the window on the port side. Through it I looked northward. It was at this time that I took several photographs.

On the starboard side of the plane was another

window. The table itself, a folding device, was Bill's chart table on which he made his calculations. Close by was the radio. Even though one could stand up in the cabin, the height of the table was such that to see out of the window one had to lean on the table or kneel beside it. There was nothing to sit on, as sitting equipment had been jettisoned to save weight.

* * *

Log Book:
> The sea for a space. Hooray. Slim has just hung a flashlight up for illuminating the compass. This light makes the radium impossible to see. Soon it will be dark enough without the flash.

* * *

The faint light of the radium instruments is almost impossible to see in dawn or twilight, when it is neither dark enough for the contrast of the radium to show nor light enough to see the numerals themselves.

* * *

Log Book:
> It is about 10. I write without light. Readable?[1]

* * *

Have you tried to write in the dark? I remember sitting up in bed at school composing themes after lights. During those night hours on the *Friendship* the log was written with the help of my good left thumb. I would not turn on the electric light in the after cabin lest it blind Bill at the controls. And so I pencilled my way across the page of the diary thankful for that early training with those better-late-than-never themes. The thumb of my left hand was used to mark the starting point of one line. The problem of this kind of blind stenography is knowing where to start the next line. It didn't always work. Too often lines piled up one on the other and legibility suffered.

* * *

Log Book:

The sea was only a respite. Fog has followed us since. We are above it now. A night of stars. North the horizon is clear cut. To the south it is a smudge.

The exhausts send out glowing meteors.

How marvellous is a machine and the mind that made it. I am thoroughly occidental in this worship.

Bill sits up alone. Every muscle and

nerve alert. Many hours to go. Marvellous also. I've driven all day and all night and know what staying alert means.

We have to climb to get over fog and roughness.

Bill gives her all she has. 5000 ft. Golly how we climb. A mountain of fog. The north star on our wing tip.

My watch says 3:15. I can see dawn to the left and still a sea of fog. We are 6000 ft. high and more. Can't read dial.

Slim and I exchange places for a while. All the dragons and sea serpents and monstrosities are silhouetted against the dawn.

9000 ft. to get over them.

The two outboard motors picked up some water a while ago. Much fuss.

At least 10,000 ft. 13 hrs. 15 min. on way.

I lose this book in Major Woolley's pockets. There are too many.

* * *

Big enough, that suit to lose myself in it. Size 40, and fur lined. It is returned now, appropriately auto-graphed. The Major has threatened to stuff and place it in a museum.

* * *

Log Book:

   Still climbing. I wish the sun would
climb up and melt these homogeneous
teddy-bears.

* * *

Beside these grotesques in the fog, which we all
remarked, there were recurrent mountains and val-
leys and countless landscapes amazingly realistic. Actually
when land itself did appear we could not be sure that
it was not an illusion too. It really took some moments
to become convinced that it was reality.

* * *

Log Book:

   Slim has just changed bats in the
flashlight hanging over the compass.

* * *

The compass was hung rather low, so far from Bill's eye
that it was difficult to read its illuminated face. So Slim
arranged a flashlight focused on it.

* * *

Log Book:

We are going down. Probably Bill is going through. Fog is lower here too. Haven't hit it yet, but soon will so far as I can see from back window....Everything shut out.

Instrument flying. Slow descent, first. Going down fast. It takes a lot to make my ears hurt. 5000 now. Awfully wet. Water dripping in window. Port motor coughing. Sounds as if all motors were cutting. Bill opens her wide to try to clear. Sounds rotten on the right.

3000 ft. Ears not so painful. Fog awful. Motors better, but not so good.

It is getting lighter and lighter as day dawns. We are not seeing it dawn, however. I wish I knew radio. I could help a lot.

We are over *² stratum now. At 3000. Bill comes back to radio to find it on the blink.

* That is the way it is written in the log book. So far no one can make out that word before "stratum." Can you? A.E.

We are running between the clouds still, but they are coming together. Many clouds all about...shouldn't bother. Port motor coughing a bit. Sounds like water.

We are going to go into, under or over a
storm. I don't like to, with one motor act-
ing the way it is.

How grey it is before; and behind, the
mass of soggy cloud we came through, is
pink with dawn. Dawn "the rosy fin-
gered," as the Odyssey has it.

Himmel! The sea! We are 3000.
Patchy clouds. We have been jazzing
from 1000 to 5000 where we now are,
to get out of clouds. At present there are
sights of blue and sunshine, but everlasting clouds always in the offing. The
radio is dead.

The sea for a while. Clouds ahead. We
ought to be coming somewhat in the
range of our destination if we are on the
course. Port motor off again. 3000 ft.
7 o'clock London.

Can't use radio at all. Coming down
now in a rather clear spot. 2500 ft.
Everything sliding forward.

8:50. 2 Boats!!!!

Trans steamer.

Try to get bearing. Radio won't. One
hr's gas. Mess. All craft cutting our
course. Why?

★ ★ ★

TAKING OFF FROM BURRY PORT, WALES

So the log ends.

Its last page records that we had but one hour's supply of gas left; that the time for reaching Ireland had
passed; that the course of the vessel sighted perplexed
us; that our radio was useless.

Where were we? Should we keep faith with our
course and continue?

"Mess" epitomized the blackness of the moment.
Were we beaten?

We all favored sticking to the course. We had to.
With faith lost in that, it was hopeless to carry on.
Besides, when last we checked it, before the radio went
dead, the plane had been holding true.

We circled the America, although having no idea
of her identity at the time. With the radio crippled, in
an effort to get our position, Bill scribbled a note. The
note and an orange to weight it, I tied in a bag with an
absurd piece of silver cord. As we circled the America,
the bag was dropped through the hatch. But the com-
bination of our speed, the movement of the vessel, the
wind and the lightness of the missile was too much for
our marksmanship. We tried another shot, using our
remaining orange. No luck.

Should we seek safety and try to come down beside
the steamer? Perhaps one reason the attempt was never
attempted was the roughness of the sea which not only
made a landing difficult but a take-off impossible.

Bill leaped to the radio with the hope of at least
receiving a message. At some moment in the excitement,

before I closed the hatch which opens in the bottom of the fuselage I lay flat and took a photograph. This, I am told, is the first one made of a vessel at sea from a plane in trans-Atlantic flight.

Then we turned back to the original course, retracing the twelve mile detour made to circle the steamer. In a way we were pooling all our chances and placing everything in a final wager on our original judgment.

Quaintly, it was this moment of lowest ebb that Slim chose to breakfast. Nonchalantly he hauled forth a sandwich.

We could see only a few miles of water, which melted into the greyness on all sides. The ceiling was so low we could fly at an altitude of only 500 feet. As we moved, our miniature world of visibility, bounded by its walls of mist, moved with us. Half an hour later into it suddenly swam a fishing vessel. In a matter of minutes a fleet of small craft, probably fishing vessels, were almost below us. Happily their course paralleled ours. Although the gasoline in the tanks was vanishing fast, we began to feel land—some land—must be near. It might not be Ireland, but any land would do just then.

Bill, of course, was at the controls. Slim, gnawing a sandwich, sat beside him, when out of the mists there grew a blue shadow, in appearance no more solid than hundreds of other nebulous "landscapes" we had sighted before. For a while Slim studied it, then turned and called Bill's attention to it.

It was land!

Can't ~~are~~ *radio at all. Coming down now in a rather clear spot. 2500 feet Everything sliding forward*

8.50 Two Boats !!! !

Trans· steamer . tried to get bearing radio wont. I hrs gas. Mrs. All craft cutting our course. Why?

PAGE FROM THE LOG BOOK

I think Slim yelled. I know the sandwich went flying out the window. Bill permitted himself a smile.

Soon several islands came into view, and then a
coast line. From it we could not determine our position, the visibility was so poor. For some time we
cruised along the edge of what we thought was typical
English countryside.

With the gas remaining, we worked along as far as
safety allowed. Bill decided to land. After circling a fac-
tory town he picked out the likeliest looking stretch and
brought the *Friendship* down in it. The only thing to tie to
was a buoy some distance away and to it we taxied.

---

[1] For reproduction of log book see page III

CHAPTER 9

JOURNEY'S END

THERE AT BURRY PORT, Wales—we learned its name later—on the morning of June 18, we opened the door of the fuselage and looked out upon what we could see of the British Isles through the rain. For Bill and Slim and me it was an introduction to the Old World. Curiously, the first crossing of the Atlantic for all of us was in the *Friendship*. None that may follow can have the quality of this initial voyage. Although we all hope to be able to cross by plane again, we have visions of doing so in a trans-Atlantic plane liner.

Slim dropped down upon the starboard pontoon and made fast to the buoy with the length of rope we had on board for just such a purpose—or, had affairs gone less well, for use with a sea anchor. We didn't doubt that tying to the buoy in such a way was against official etiquette and that shortly we should be reprimanded by some marine traffic cop. But the buoy was the only mooring available and as we'd come rather a long way, we risked offending.

We could see factories in the distance and hear the hum of activity. Houses dotted the green hillside. We were some distance off shore but the beach looked muddy and barren. The only people in sight were three men working on a railroad track at the base of the hill. To them we waved, and Slim yelled lustily for service.

Finally they noticed us, straightened up and even went so far as to walk down to the shore and look us over. Then their animation died out and they went back to their work. The *Friendship* simply wasn't interesting. An itinerant trans-Atlantic plane meant nothing.

In the meantime three or four more people had gathered to look at us. To Slim's call for a boat we had no answer. I waved a towel desperately out the front windows and one friendly soul pulled off his coat and waved back.

It must have been nearly an hour before the first boats came out. Our first visitor was Norman Fisher who arrived in a dory. Bill went ashore with him and telephoned our friends at Southampton while Slim and I remained on the *Friendship*. A vigorous ferry service was soon instituted and many small boats began to swarm about us. While we waited Slim contrived a nap. I recall I seriously considered the problem of a sandwich and decided food was not interesting just then.

Late in the afternoon Captain Railey, whom I had last seen in Boston, arrived by seaplane with Captain

Bailey of the Imperial Airways and Allen Raymond of the New York Times.

Owing to the racing tide, it was decided not to try to take off but to leave the plane at Burry Port and stay at a nearby hotel for the night. Bill made a skilful mooring in a protected harbor and we were rowed ashore. There were six policemen to handle the crowd. That they got us through was remarkable. In the enthusiasm of their greeting those hospitable Welsh people nearly tore our clothes off.

Finally we reached the shelter of the Frickers Metal Company office where we remained until police reinforcements arrived. In the meantime we had tea and I knew I was in Britain.

Twice, before the crowd would let us get away, we had to go to an upper balcony and wave. They just wanted to see us. I tried to make them realize that all the credit belonged to the boys, who did the work. But from the beginning it was evident the accident of sex—the fact that I happened to be the first woman to have made the Atlantic flight—made me the chief performer in our particular sideshow.

With the descent of reporters one of the first questions I was asked was whether I knew Colonel Lindbergh and whether I thought I looked like him. Gleefully they informed me I had been dubbed "Lady Lindy." I explained that I had never had the honor of meeting Colonel Lindbergh, that I was sure I looked like no one (and, just then, nothing) in the world, and that I would grasp the first opportunity to apologize to him for innocently inflicting the idiotic comparison. (The idiotic part is all mine, of course.)

The celebration began with interviews and photographs. We managed to have dinner and what was most comforting of all, hot baths. The latter were high-lights of our reception, being the first experience of the kind since leaving Boston weeks—or was it months?—previously.

Sleep that night was welcome. In all, we had five or six hours. We could not rest the next day, because an early start was necessary in order to reach Southampton on schedule.

Rain and mist in the morning, that finally cleared somewhat, allowed us to take off. We skimmed over Bristol Channel and the green hills of Devonshire, which were as beautiful as we had imagined. In the plane with the crew were Captain Railey and Mr. Raymond of the Times.

When we set out from Burry Port on this last lap of the journey, Captain Bailey of the Imperial Airways had expected to guide us. Unfortunately at the last moment he was unable to start his engine and Bill decided to hop for Southampton unescorted.

As we approached, a seaplane came out to meet us, and we presumed it was to guide us to the landing place. As Bill prepared to follow, Captain Railey discovered that we were not being guided. In the uncertainty of landing amid berthed steamers in a strange place, Bill finally picked up the green lights

LEAVING BURRY PORT, WALES

of a signal gun which marked the official launch coming to greet us. Mrs. Guest, owner of the *Friendship*, and
sponsor of the flight, was there, her son Raymond, and
Hubert Scott Payne of the Imperial Airways. My first
meeting with the generous woman who permitted me
so much, was there in Southampton. It was a rather
exciting moment despite the fatigue which was creep-
ing upon all of us. On shore we were welcomed by Mrs.
Foster Welch, the Mayor of Southampton. She wore
her official necklace in honor of the occasion and we
were impressed with her graciousness. Though a
woman may hold such office in Great Britain, the fact

isn't acknowledged, for she is still addressed as if she were a man.

With the crowd behind, I drove to London with Mr. and Mrs. Scott Payne. The whole ride seemed a dream. I remember stopping to see Winchester Cathedral and hearing that Southampton was the only seaplane base in England and being made to feel really at home by Mrs. Payne, who sat next to me.

London gave us so much to do and see that I hardly had time to think. One impression lingers,—that of warm hospitality which was given without stint. I stayed with Mrs. Guest at Park Lane. Lady Astor permitted me a glance of beautiful country when she invited me to Cliveden. Lord Lonsdale was host at the Olympic Horse Show, which happened to be in action during our stay. The British Air League were hosts at a large luncheon primarily organized by the women's division at which I was particularly glad to meet Madame de Landa and Lady Heath. From the latter I bought the historic little Avro with which she had flown alone from Cape Town to London. I was guest, too, at a luncheon of Mrs. Houghton's, wife of the American Ambassador—and many other people lavished undeserved hospitality upon us.

Being a social worker I had of course to see Toynbee Hall, dean of settlement houses, on which our own Denison House in Boston is patterned. Nothing in England will interest me more than to revisit Toynbee Hall and the settlement houses that I did not see.

But this can be no catalogue of what that brief time in London meant to us. To attempt to say "thank you" adequately would take a book in itself—and this little volume is to concern the flight and whatever I may be able to add about aviation in general. Altogether it was an alluring introduction to England, enough to make me wish to return and explore, what this time, I merely touched.

Before we left, the American correspondents invited me to a luncheon—another of the pleasant memories of our visit. It was "not for publication." And although I was the only woman present we talked things over, I think, on a real man-to-man basis. From first to last my contact with the press has been thoroughly enjoyable; in England and in America I could not possibly ask for greater cooperation, sincerity, and genuine friendliness.

On June 28 we began our first ocean voyage, embarking on the S.S. President Roosevelt of the United States Lines, commanded by Captain Harry Manning. It really was our first ocean voyage and it was then that we came to realize how much water we had passed over in the *Friendship*. Eastbound the mileage had been measured over clouds, not water. There never had been adequate comprehension of the Atlantic below us.

A curious connection exists between the Roosevelt and the America. Not only had the Roosevelt relayed some of our radio messages, but Captain Fried of the America had formally been skipper of the Roosevelt.

EARHART, STULTZ, GORDON, AND LOCAL PRESS
IMMEDIATELY AFTER LANDING IN BURRY PORT

It was Captain Fried who figured so finely in the heroic rescue of the sinking freighter Antinoe a couple of years ago. Captain Fried, I was told, is interested in trans-Atlantic flight projects. On the America he makes it a practice, when he knows a flight is in progress, to have painted periodically the ship's position on the hatches in such a way that the information may be read by a plane passing overhead. On the day when we saw the America he had received no news of our flight so that preparations had not been made for the usual hatch-painting. Actually, however, if we had remained above the America perhaps a few more minutes the information we sought would have been painted on her decks, ending our uncertainties at once. As it was, Capt. Fried cabled us on board the Roosevelt that the operator had called "plane, plane"—not knowing our letters, in an effort to give us our bearings. But Bill could not pick up the word.

When the Roosevelt reached quarantine in New York, she was held there several hours until the Mayor's yacht Macon arrived with its officials, its bands, and our friends. I was sorry to delay other passengers in the Roosevelt who had breakfasted at six and who were forced to wait while we were welcomed.

Then up the bay, to the City Hall and to the Biltmore. Interviews, photographs, and medals, and best of all, friends.

We were home again, with one adventure behind and, as always in this life, others ahead.

CHAPTER 10

AVIATION INVITES

THE RECEPTION GIVEN US—and accorded the flyers who preceded us—indicates, it seems to me, the increasing air-mindedness of America. And it is not only air-expeditions, pioneer explorations and "stunts" which command attention.

The air mail, perhaps more than any other branch of aeronautics, has brought home to the average man realization of the possibilities of aviation. Its regularity and dependability are taken for granted by many. While our development of this phase of air transport is notable, the United States is somewhat backward in other branches, compared with the European nations. We lag behind the procession in passenger carrying and the number of privately owned planes, in proportion to our size.

Abroad, the entire industry is generously subsidized by the various governments. Of course, aviation here knows no such support, a fact which means that, so far as we have gone, our industry is on a sound basis economically.

Although air transport in the U. S. A. has had to pay its own way, and is behind somewhat, slightly over 2000 commercial airplanes were constructed in 1927, and operations in the field of mail and transport flying approximated 6,000,000 miles flown. Nearly nine thousand passengers were carried, and two and a half million pounds of freight transported.

Impressive as are these figures, they are not comparable to the volume inevitable.

When I am asked what individuals can do to aid aviation my reply is, to those who haven't flown: "Fly." For, whether or not aviation will be found useful in their lives, or whether they find flying pleasant, at least they will have some understanding of what it is, if they go up. Every day all of us have opportunity to do our bit—and to get our bit—by using the air for our long-distance mail, and at least some of our express and freight. And perhaps some who come to touch aviation in these ways, will find an interest which will carry them into the ranks of plane owners.

Most people have quite incorrect ideas about the sensation of flying. Their mental picture of how it feels to go up in a plane is based on the way the plane looks when it takes off and flies, or upon their amusement-park experience in a roller-coaster. Some of the uninitiated compare flying to the memory of the last time they peered over the edge of a high building. The sensation of such moments is almost entirely lacking in a plane. Flying is so matter-of-fact that probably the passenger taking off for the first time will not know when he has left the ground.

I heard a man say as he left a plane after his first trip, "Well, the most remarkable thing about flying is that it isn't remarkable."

The sensation which accompanies height, for instance, so much feared by the prospective air passenger, is seldom present. There is no tangible connection between the plane and the earth, as there is in the case of a high building. To look at the street from a height of twenty stories gives some an impulse to jump. In the air, the passenger hasn't that feeling of absolute height, and he can look with perfect equanimity at the earth below. An explanation is that with the high building there is an actual contact between the body of the observer and the ground, creating a feeling of height. The plane passenger has no longer any vertical solid connecting him with the ground— and the atmosphere which fills the space between the bottom of the plane and the earth doesn't have the same effect.

Many people seem to think that going up in the air will have some ill effect on their hearts. I know a woman who was determined to die of heart failure if she made a flight. She isn't logical, for she rolls lazily through life encased in 100 lbs. of extra avoirdupois, which surely adds a greater strain on her heart—besides not giving it any fun, at all.

Seriously, of course a person with a chronically weak heart, who is affected by altitude, should not invite trouble by flying. A lame man should exercise special care in crossing a street with crowded traffic, and one with weak lungs should not attempt swimming a long distance unaccompanied.

Consciousness of speed in the air is surprisingly absent. Thirty miles an hour in an automobile, or fifty in a railroad train, gives one greater sensation of speed than moving one hundred miles an hour in a large plane. On the highway every pebble passed is a speedometer for one's eye, while the ties and track whirling backward from an observation car register the train's motion.

In the air there are no stones or trees or telegraph poles—no milestones for the eye, to act as speed indicators. Only a somewhat flattened countryside below, placidly slipping away or spreading out. Even when the plane's velocity is greatly altered no noticeable change in the whole situation ensues—80 miles an hour at several thousand feet is substantially the same as 140, so far as the sensations of sight and feeling are concerned.

Piloting differs from driving a car in that there is an added necessity for lateral control. An automobile runs up and down hill, and turns left or right. A plane climbs or dives, turns, and in addition, tips from one side to another. There is no worry in a car about whether the two left wheels are on the road or not; but a pilot must normally keep his wings level. Of course doing so becomes as automatic as driving straight, but is, nevertheless, dependent upon senses ever alert.

One of the first things a student learns in flying, is that he turns by pushing a rudder bar the way he wants to go. (The little wagons of our youth turned opposite the push, remember?)

When he turns he must bank or tip the wings at the same time. Why? Because the plane would skid in exactly the same way a car does if it whirls around a level corner.

The inside of an automobile race track is like a bowl, with the sides growing steeper toward the top. The cars climb toward the outer edge in proportion to their speed, and it is quite impossible to force a slow car up the steep side of the bowl. The faster it goes the steeper the bank must be and the sharper the turn. A pilot must make his own "bowl" and learn to tip his plane the right degree relative to the sharpness of his turn and his speed. A skid means lack of control, for a while, either on the ground or in the air, and of course is to be avoided. By the way, compensating for skidding is the same with a car or plane—one turns either craft in the direction of the skid.

Besides skidding, a plane can stall exactly as a car does on a hill. The motor is overtaxed and stops. The plane motor doesn't stop, but just as a stalled car starts to roll backwards down the hill, so the stalled plane begins to drop. Recovery of control with an automobile is simple; only a matter of jamming on the breaks and getting the engine started again. With the plane there is similarly little difficulty; it falls for a moment until it attains enough forward speed to make the rudder and elevators again effective. This is comparable to the ineffectiveness of a rudder on a too slow-moving boat. If a plane stall with out motor occurs so close to the earth that there isn't time to recover control, a hard landing results.

But in the air, as with automobiles, most accidents are due to the human equation. The careful driver, either below or aloft, barring the hard luck of mechanical failure, has remarkably little trouble, considering what he has to contend with.

I think it is a fair statement that for the average landing, the descent of the plane is less noticeable than the dropping of the modern high-speed elevator. It comes down in a gentle glide at an angle often much less than that of a country hill. As a result, unless a passenger is actually watching for the landing, he is aware he is approaching the ground only when the motors are idled.

"I would gladly fly if we could stay very close to the ground," is a statement that I have heard often in one way or another. As a matter of fact, a plane 100 feet off the earth is in infinitely more danger than one 3600 feet aloft.

Trouble in the air is very rare. It is hitting the ground that causes it. Obviously the higher one

ON THE ROOF OF THE HYDE PARK HOTEL, LONDON

happens to be, the more time there is to select a safe landing place in case of difficulty. For a ship doesn't fall like a plummet, even if the engine goes dead. It assumes a natural gliding angle which sometimes is as great as eight to one. That is, a plane 5000 feet in the air can travel in any direction eight times its altitude (40,000 feet) or practically eight miles. Thus it has a potential landing radius of 16 miles.

Sometimes, a cautious pilot elects to come down at once to make a minor engine adjustment. Something is wrong and he, properly, is unwilling to risk flying further, even though probably able to do so. Just so the automobile driver, instead of limping on with, say, worn distributor points, or a foul spark plug, would do well to stop at once at a garage and get his engine back into efficient working order.

All of which obviously points to the necessity of providing frequent landing places along all airways. Few things, I think, would do more to eliminate accidents in the air. With perfected motors the dread of forced landings will be forgotten, and with more fields, at least in the populous areas, "repair" landings would be safe and easy.

Eliminating many of the expected sensations of flying doesn't mean that none are to be anticipated or that those left are only pleasant. There are poor days for flying as well as good ones. Just as in yachting, weather plays an important part, and sometimes entirely prevents a trip. Even ocean liners are occasionally held over in port to avoid a storm, or are prevented from making a scheduled landing because of adverse conditions. In due time a plane will probably become as reliable as these ocean vessels of today, because although a severe storm will wreck it, its greater speed will permit it to fly around the storm area—to escape dangers rather than battle through them as a ship must do.

The choppy days at sea have a counterpart in what flyers call "bumpy" conditions over land. Air is liquid flow and where obstructions occur there will be eddies. For instance, imagine wind blowing directly toward a clump of trees, or coming in sudden contact with a cliff or steep mountain. Water is thrown up when it strikes against a rock and just so is a stream of air broken on the object in its way, and diverted upward in atmospheric gusts which correspond to the spray of the seaside. Encountering such a condition a plane gets a "wallop"—is tossed up and buffeted as it rolls over the wave.

There are bumps, too, from sources other than these land shoals. Areas of cool air and warm disturb the flow of aerial rivers through which the plane moves. The "highs" and "lows" familiar to the meteorologists—the areas of high and low barometric pressure—are forever playing tag with each other, the air from one area flowing in upon the other much as water seeks its own level, creating fair weather and foul, and offering interesting problems to the students of avigation, not to mention variegated experiences to the flyer himself.

The nautical boys have an advantage over the aviators. Constant things like the gulf stream can be labeled and put on charts and shoals marked. But one can't fasten buoys in the atmosphere. Flyers can only plot topography. Air, like water, gives different effects under different conditions. The pilot must learn that when the wind blows over a hill from one direction, the result is not the same as that when it blows from another. Water behaves similarly. The shoals of the air seem a little more elusive, however, because their eddies are invisible. If one could see a downward current of air or a rough patch of it, avigating might be easier sometimes.

"Bumpiness" means discomfort, or a good time for strong stomachs, in the air just as rough water does in ocean voyaging. There is no reason to suppose, however, if one isn't susceptible to seasickness or carsickness, that air travel will prove different.

Some of the air-sickness experienced is due to the lack of proper ventilation in cabin planes. Many are not adequately ventilated for with the opening of the windows, the heat and sometimes the fumes of the motors are blown in. Adequate ventilation is one of the amenities which the plane of the future will have to possess.

Perhaps the greatest joy of flying is the magnificent extent of the view. If the visibility is good, the passenger seems to see the whole world.

I have spoken of the effect of height in flattening the landscape, always a phenomenon in the eyes of the air novitiate. Even mountains grow humble and a really rough terrain appears comparatively smooth. Trees look like bushes, and automobiles like flat-backed bugs. A second plane which may be flying a few hundred feet above the ground, as seen from a greater altitude looks as if it were just skimming the surface. All vertical measurement is fore-shortened.

The world seen from the air is laid out in squares. Especially striking is the checkerboard effect wherever one looks down on what his brother man has done. Country or city, it is the same—only the rectangles are of different sizes. The city plays its game of checkers in smaller spaces than the country, and divides its area more minutely.

If one is fortunate enough to fly over clouds, another world is entered. The clouds may be grey or white or tinted the exquisite colors of sunset. Sometimes "holes" occur in them through which little glimpses of the earth may be seen. It is possible to be lying in sunshine and to look down on a piece of dull grey earth. There is sport to be had playing hide-and-seek through the light fluffy clouds that are not compact enough to be ominous. An instant of greyness is followed by a flash of sunlight as one emerges into the clear air. By the way, a flyer can dissipate a fairly small cloud by diving into it.

That is the fun of the clouds which look like "mashed potatoes." The big fellows can be much more serious. Once into them, and one has the sensation of being surrounded by an everlasting mass of grey, comparable, so far as visibility goes, with a heavy fog. In such clouds one can find all varieties of weather—rain, snow, or sleet.

In the trans-Atlantic flight, we encountered both rain and snow. There lies one of the greatest risks of long distance flying—I mean moisture freezing upon the wings of the plane. The danger zone of temperature is said to lie chiefly between twenty-four and thirty-eight degrees, when slush begins to form. Once in trouble of that kind, the pilot does his best to find warmer or colder temperature, normally by decreasing or increasing his altitude.

CHATTING WITH AN ENGLISH BOBBY

As an example of the ice menace, I was told of a plane which after a very few moments in the air was barely able to regain the field whence it had taken off in a sleet storm, coming down with a coating of ice which weighed at least five hundred pounds.

Speaking of ice, I am often asked about the temperatures in the air. "Is it dreadfully cold up there?"

Recently a group flew from New York to Boston on one of the hottest mornings of the summer. The temperatures at about 2000 feet were probably some degrees lower than those prevailing on the ground. We all know that unless one encounters a breeze, often the temperature on a mountain 5000 feet high is no more agreeable than that at its base. In a small open plane, as contrasted to the cabin ship, one would have a pleasanter time on a summer day, and conversely more discomfort in cold weather. It parallels the experience in an open car.

In crossing the Atlantic I think the lowest temperature we had in the unheated aft cabin of the *Friendship* was around forty. Our lowest outside temperatures were only a few degrees below this. On the Atlantic our maximum altitude was about 11,000 feet, with an average far lower. Doubtless it would have been colder had we flown high more of the distance.

In addition to the visual joys of airscapes, there is much else that flying gives. Nothing, perhaps, is more appealing than the sense of quick accomplishment—of getting somewhere, sooner. Aviation means an approach to the elimination of time wastage, and seems to point the way to further increase in the world's leisure.

Humanity reaches for leisure—as time in which to do what it wants. The Orient finds contemplation its pleasure, while the Occident is not content without action. Of course, Americans are noted for the work they do to play. Perhaps aviation will tend to make them enjoy life a little more, by providing time to do something else.

CHAPTER II

WOMEN IN AVIATION

WHILE THIS CHAPTER is called "Women in Aviation," just as appropriate a title might have been "Women Outside of Aviation." For women really to influence aviation development it is not essential that they be flyers themselves, although the more who fly the better. When the women of America are thoroughly "sold" on aviation, not only as a sporting phenomenon but as an everyday utility, air transport will come into its own.

Today we have planes for carrying passengers, mail, express and freight. It is the modern note in transportation, comparable to the electric refrigerator, vacuum devices and all the other leisure making appliances of the household. Aviation is another time-saver ready to be utilized.

Generally speaking, women control the purchasing power of the modern economic world. It is a brave man who buys another make when his wife wants a

Chrysler! Woman's influence primarily is responsible for the rapid development of the American automobile's beauty and comfort. A similar influence inevitably will be exerted in connection with air transport—*if women will fly.* As they become an important factor in passenger revenue their requirements will be increasingly studied and met.

Conversely, it is my opinion that if the show windows of aviation were made more attractive women in far larger numbers would be lured into the air. Specifically, I mean landing fields and their appurtenances. The average field today is a comfortless place. Too often its approaches and its equipment are uninviting. It attracts nobody except people who have to go there.

The time is coming, I think, when all the fields will be attractive and convenient. When they are, it will be easier to procure feminine backing. As it is now, the only thing attractive to feminine eyes, in many flying fields is the handsome collection of flyers.

Besides flying there is much that women can do in the various branches of the industry. Many touch it now in factories, offices, fields, service stations and the like. In such jobs it is ability, not sex, which counts, in the final analysis.

There should be no line between men and women, so far as piloting is concerned. Except when the muscular strength of men is a deciding factor, it hardly seems possible great differences exist. Of course, so few women have essayed flying that no comparison of ability can justly be made yet. In them even the desire to learn to fly must be cultivated so the only possible criterion is that of their driving. Bring on the arguments.

Age and physical equipment determine the fitness to fly. While there are many older people learning to fly today, and many excellent pilots who are no longer young, still it is youth which has the advantage, as in all physical activities.

I make no statement as to how young youth is. To soothe excitable mothers, I should say, they needn't worry yet about children under seven adding to life's complexities by trying to fly, and that pilots' licenses can't be obtained after fifty-two.

Today there are ample facilities for flying instruction throughout the United States. It is, however, considerably more difficult for a woman to procure it than it is for a man. A primary reason is the advantage a man has through what the army and the navy offer. By enlisting in either branch the beginner has not only free instruction but actually receives a salary as well and in due course many emerge as a competent pilot. There is no such opening for women. She must pay for the instruction she gets.

And it is just a little harder, too, for the woman to get this instruction at the average field than it is for the man. It is not so much that there is any definite prejudice against the woman beginner—the men are remarkably fair in their attitude—but that as matters stand, it is pretty well a man-conducted business.

Equipment too is naturally designed for men—
for instance, there is no parachute really adequate for
women. Woman is conscious that she is intruding—or
something akin to that—a feeling which causes hesita-
tion. That same sort of thing prevails in medicine, the
law, and other professions, to a certain degree. Gradually
it is being overcome where ability has been demonstrated. Too often, I think, sex has been used as a sub-
terfuge by the inefficient woman who likes to make
herself and others believe that it is not her incapabil-
ity, but her womanhood, which is holding her back.

Generally speaking, the average cost of ten hours
in the air, as I have said, is about $250. But ten hours
in the air doesn't make a finished pilot. After such time
the average person should be able to solo, but it is experience which alone counts. A novice can learn to drive
an automobile in a way in a matter of a few hours, but
only mileage makes him competent.

New planes can be bought for a little more than
$2000 and up. Hangar space comes to from twenty-
five to fifty dollars a month and up. Obviously a very
large plane will cost more to store and handle than a
small one. A plaything with a wing spread of seventy-
two feet, such as *Friendship* had, requires as much space
as a whole fleet of trucks, and specialized space at that.
It is not simply a matter of a building in which to
house the plane. There should be a well equipped
field outside, with runways, lights, and facilities rang-
ing all the way from a filling station to a machine

shop. And for all of this overhead one naturally has to pay. The actual cost of plane maintenance depends entirely upon the amount of use made of it, exactly as with an automobile. I don't believe any reliable estimates of upkeep are available.

The number of hours a motor can run, without overhauling, depends not only on the motor itself but the character of the attention given it. Meticulous care of a plane's power plant is vital. It is not that the motors themselves are any more complicated than the engines of large automobiles, but there simply aren't any service stations 10,000 feet in the air. An oversight on a highway means only inconvenience; one aloft means inconvenience, too—the inconvenience of coming down where there may be a landing field or there may not.

All of which information may sound indefinite. But I believe exactly the same uncertainty applies to automobiling. Few people who have one or two cars can say exactly what a year's operation costs, when depreciation, replacement and performance are figured. The cost of upkeep of any machine depends in a great measure upon the amount of time the owner himself devotes, or has devoted, to its care and the degree of skill employed. Withal, I believe that the maintenance of a plane is probably very little greater than that of a similarly priced automobile.

There is a belief, I suppose (and perhaps it is well founded) that women shrink more than do men from the alleged hazards of aviation. Inheritance, training and environment seem to make women less aggressive than men, although in real courage I think they are equals. So much of woman's excitement through the ages has been pushing the men into adventure that they have the habit of hanging back a little. We can't infer Lady Macbeth lacked courage or ability because she herself didn't do the job she wanted Macbeth to do.

Regarding flying risks, as compared to others, there is an endless field for discussion. Figures as to accidents and flying hours mileage I have quoted elsewhere. I know the facts and the conclusions to be drawn from them remain largely a matter of individual opinion. But whether one feels flying fairly safe or not it must be admitted it is safer than it was. Recent steps have been made in securing true safety for the flyer in the last few years. Once attainment of something akin to it was merely a vague hope. If one flew one took the risks. Selah.

The problems of safety are concerned with the engineering problem of the motor and design of the plane, the skill of the pilot and ground technique. Probably improvements in the power units will always be made. But it seems impossible that advances can go on so rapidly as they have in the last few years. It has been well demonstrated recently that the multiple engine plane has a factor of safety far beyond what is possible with the single engine.

The *Friendship* is equipped with three. If one motor fails the other two can carry on, even with the large gas supply for long-distance flying aboard. At the end of a flight, when a minimum load weight has been reached, it is possible with one motor to keep the plane in the air. One engine can also greatly prolong the downward glide of the crippled plane for a forced landing, if need be. For instance, in flying over the ocean if two motors had cut out simultaneously (an unlikely contingency), with the remaining one the plane could have continued much farther than it could have, without any. The power of one motor would have made possible a flatter, and thus more extensive, glide. That long glide might enable one to reach a ship lane, or specifically, come down in the vicinity of some particular vessel that had been located by radio in the meantime.

The plane and the engine, of course, are no better than their pilot. His reliability and skill are essential. There are fine men in the game today and on their capable shoulders the success of flying leans heavily.

Just as the railway accumulated air-breaks, automatic signals, etc., so is the aeroplane being improved with safety devices. Landing places are included under this head. Their frequency is important, as well as their conduct. Some fields are so congested that planes have to circle about for minutes before rules of the air allow them to land. Terminal operations will have to be worked out as thoroughly as they have been by railroads and the safety devices of airways—lights, radio, signals, etc.—be equally efficient.

Despite the fact that there are traffic laws to govern flying, and inspectors to enforce them, many infringements occur. Bad manners of the air exist, unfortunately, as they do on the automobile highways or on the high seas. Any maneuver which endangers another's life needlessly, no matter where, seems to me bad manners. The pilot who flies low over crowds or stunts near the ground, I fear, is not quite playing the game. His misdemeanors can be reported to the police and his license number given just as can be an offending automobile driver.

Most pilots are careful of such breaches of etiquette for their reputation counts. There are some who overstep, and there will be a few accidents caused by them from time to time, until they gradually are reformed.

Possibly that feature of aviation which may appeal most to thoughtful women is its potentiality for peace. The term is not merely an airy phrase.

Isolation breeds distrust and differences of outlook. Anything which tends to annihilate distance destroys isolation, and brings the world and its peoples closer together. I think aviation has a chance to increase intimacy, understanding, and far-flung friendships thus.

CHAPTER 12

PROBLEMS AND PROGRESS

IT WOULD BE WRONG to attempt to lure people into the air with any false assurances that everything connected with aviation runs like clock-work. It doesn't. Because the whole industry is so new it probably has more difficulties proportionately than many others. Growing pains are inevitable. Aviation is only now emerging into the status of an industry. Hitherto it has been largely a jumble of gallant individual efforts. Even today, there are more independent producers of airplanes than there are automobile manufacturers. The survival of the fittest, with accompanying combinations, will come just as they have come in the motor industry.

Most present-day manufacturers are swamped with orders. Eventually the better products will survive. In plane buying the same sort of selection as prevails with automobiles—that is, that based on quality—will become effective.

WILMER STULTZ, AMELIA EARHAT, AND LOUIS "SLIM"
GORDON WAVING IN NEW YORK PARADE

No thoughtful person associated with aviation makes any claims as to the infallibility of air equipment. Of course there are accidents. The surprising part is not how many, but how few, there are.[1]

ACCIDENTS AND THEIR CAUSES

Planes Involved in Accidents
Licensed..34
Unlicensed...<u>166</u> 200

Pilots Involved in Accidents
Licensed pilots....................................35
Unlicensed pilots..............................<u>165</u> 200

Probable Causes of Accidents
Pilots...34
Mechanical defects........................43
Structural failure..........................23
Weather..12
Other causes...................................14
Unknown...<u>8</u> 200

There is an element of unfairness in comparing mechanical failures and human errors on the ground, with those in the air. The results are so different—*as matters stand today.* An automobile engine gives out. Normally the worst that happens is a stalled car, and some resulting inconvenience. Even if a wheel comes off the damage, and danger, is comparatively slight. But let an accident of similar magnitude occur in the air, and the consequences may be serious. Serious, that is, unless there is a landing field in reachable distance. And

Kinds of Flying Engaged In

Miscellaneous............................. 139
Student.................................. 23
Experimental (including tran-oceanic). 23
Demonstration.......................... 3
Air transport............................ 12   200

Fatalities-Various Causes

Pilots..................................... 79
Mechanical defects..................... 22
Structural failure........................ 22
Weather................................. 9
Other causes............................ 13
Unknown................................ 19   164

Fatalities in Post-Office Air Mail Operations

Calendar Year	Miles	Fatalities		Miles per Fatality
		Pilots	Passengers	
1927	1,413,381	1	0	1,413,381
1926	2,583,056	1	0	2,583,056
1925	2,521,758	1	0	2,521,758
1924	2,161,077	3	0	720,359
1923	1,870,422	5	1	347,084
1922	1,756,803	1	0	1,756,803
1921	1,912,733	7	2	273,248
1920	1,048,444	8	6	74,886
1919	461,295	4	0	115,324
1918	102,548	1	0	102,548
Total...	15,831,517	32	9	....

therein lies an outstanding problem of American aviation development.

During 1927 there were 482 municipal and commercial fields in the United States, with 56 under construction. In addition there were 53 army and 8 navy fields. Taking the whole lot, and adding the comparatively few in Canada and Mexico, it gives a pretty thin coverage for the continent.

While it is true that in some parts of the country, notably in the level areas of the west, one can land with safety almost anywhere, it is necessary to have service as well as landing facilities. Obviously adequately equipped fields will follow the economic justification for them. And that justification is fast approaching.

Too often cities have delayed in purchasing land for air terminal facilities. Acreage near a population center was either not available or too expensive. Many landing fields, excellent in themselves, are so remote that the primary appeal of flying, namely, its time-saving element, is hopelessly offset by the waste of time in getting to and from the airport.

Notable among the cities attacking the problems is Chicago. A five million dollar bond issue is being put through there which will finance the creation of a model airport. It will be situated close to the very heart of the city itself, actually only ten or fifteen minutes by automobile from Chicago's business center. This is in contrast to the forty or fifty minutes required to reach the present municipal field. Chicago's lead may well be followed by other American cities—although, of course, a number are already well equipped.

Hind-sight is so easy—and so costly. If, for instance, in the development of our larger cities, especially the comparatively new towns of the middle western states, we had been able to visualize the present day requirements of the automobile, how easily modern traffic problems could have been prepared for. All our cities have faced the experience and the expense of widening streets already built; and all of them are shadowboxing with the unsolvable puzzle of forcing a thousand automobiles through inadequate thoroughfares designed to handle perhaps a hundred facilely.

It is possible, of course, that long runways won't be necessary for the aircraft of the future. Science may teach us how to alight and take off from very small areas, such as the tops of buildings. Even if such events do eventually come to pass, there will be plenty of meantime for the cities to reap reward for their investments in landing fields. At the worst, in after years what a generous gesture it would be for the municipalities to plan to turn these unused fields into playgrounds for the derelicts whose mentality has finally snapped under the strain of a too enthusiastic promotion of aviation!

Just another word about fields—a word of warning, if you will. A great many communities, even really small ones, can support and will be benefited by landing fields. But the smaller community should not strain its resources trying to create elaborate airports, for which economic support reasonably cannot be expected. After all, the field, if adequate in area, can grow into an airport.

EARHART AND *FRIENDSHIP* PILOT WILMER STULTZ

The activities of the Department of Commerce are admirably summarized in the Air Craft Year Book published by the Aeronautical Chamber of Commerce of America, from which the following paragraphs are quoted:

"Civil aeronautics made great progress during the first year of Federal cooperation and supervision under the Air Commerce Act of 1926, efficiently administered by the Department of Commerce, under the direction of Assistant Secretary William P. MacCracken. New airways were laid out, lighted and mapped. Improved lighting equipment was developed and installed. Many municipalities with Federal encouragement and assistance other than monetary established adequate airports. Airway bulletins containing airport maps and information were published and distributed. Radio aids to avigation passed through their laboratory tests and started on service tests. Plans for better aeronautical weather service have been formulated and partially installed.

"Undoubtedly the outstanding accomplishment of the year was the promulgation and enforcement of the air commerce regulations with practically no friction or upheaval, at a time when the industry itself was undergoing tremendous expansion....

"One of the greatest problems confronting the Department of Commerce in its aeronautical duties was to secure adequate appropriations. Civil aeronautics in this country is being successfully developed without Government subsidy, but this does not mean that the Federal Government will not have to spend large sums of money for aids to avigation, and to promote the use of aircraft in commerce...

"One of the most interesting problems has been that of organization. The Air Commerce Act provided comprehensively for the promotion and regulation of civil aeronautics, but it did not create a new bureau in the Department of Commerce to perform the functions. The intention was that so far as practicable, the duties imposed by the act should be distributed among existing agencies of the department.

"Accordingly, the task of establishing, maintaining and operating aids to avigation along air routes was assigned to the Lighthouse Service; the mapping of air routes, to the Coast and Geodetic Survey; the scientific research for the improvement of air navigation aids, to the Bureau of Standards; and the development of foreign market to the Bureau of Foreign and Domestic Commerce.

"The department had no facilities for the examination and licensing of aircraft and airmen, for the enforcement of air traffic rules, or for the collection and dissemination of aeronautical information. It was necessary to set up new instrumentalities to deal with these matters, and two special divisions were accordingly established—the Division of Air Regulations and the Division of Air Information. For convenience of reference these two divisions, together with the Airways Division of the Bureau of Lighthouses, the Airway Mapping Section of the Coast and Geodetic Survey, and the Aeronautical Research Division of the Bureau of Standards, are collectively referred to as the Aeronautics Branch of the Department.

"The work of the Air Regulations Division includes the inspection of aircraft for airworthiness and their registration as aircraft of the United States; the examination and licensing of airmen serving in connection with licensed aircraft; the identification by letter and number of all aircraft, including those not licensed; the investigation of accidents and the enforcement of air traffic rules....

"It is contemplated that practically all new pro-

ADDRESSING THE CROWD AT NEW YORK'S CITY HALL

duction aircraft will be manufactured under what is known as an approved type certificate. In order to secure such a certificate the manufacturer submits to the Air Regulation Division plans and specifications with a stress analysis. This is checked by aeronautical engineers and if found satisfactory an airplane built according to these specifications is then given a thorough flight test. After this has been successfully accomplished the certificate is issued. Thereafter planes manufactured according to the approved plans and specifications will be licensed upon the manufacturer's affidavit to this effect and a short flight test. The department's aircraft inspectors and aeronautical engineers visit the various factories from time to time to check up on materials and workmanship, but Government inspectors are not stationed regularly at any of the factories.

"To carry out the medical certification of applicants there have been 230 doctors appointed in various parts of the country, all of whom operate under the medical director of the Aeronautics Branch.

"Pilots receive identification cards and licenses when they have satisfactorily passed their medical, piloting and intelligence tests. The license is renewable periodically, depending upon the class in which it has been issued. These classes include the air transport, limited commercial, industrial, private and student pilot licenses. Each calls for different qualifications, all of which are explained in the Air Commerce Regulations.

"Aircraft are registered in classes according to weight. All craft which operate in interstate commerce or in the furtherance of a business which includes interstate commerce are required to be licensed. All aircraft whether operating in interstate commerce non-commercially or solely within a State must bear identification numbers issued by the department and must obey the air traffic rules contained in the Air Commerce Regulations.

"The Department of Commerce keeps in touch constantly with activities of the manufacturers and of the aerial service and transport operators by means of periodical surveys. These surveys reveal that during 1927 a total of 2,011 commercial airplanes were constructed, with unfilled orders for 907 planes, representing a total value of $12,502,405. The operations in the field by the commercial flyers approximate 13,000,000 miles of flying; 500,000 passengers carried, and 2,500,000 pounds of freight and express transported.

"The Airways Division selects and establishes intermediate landing fields and installs and maintains lighting equipment and other aids to avigation on established airways. In addition, it is charged with the establishment of radio aids, maintenance of a weather reporting service and a general communication system throughout the airways.

"The field service now consists of 20 airway extension superintendents, all-pilots, 11 inspectors, 6 engineers, 4 mechanics, and in addition, numerous radio operators, caretakers and weather observers, at intermediate fields and in some cases at beacon lights."

The air problems of the army and navy are peculiar to themselves. Governmental support is naturally important in the development of planes and motors and in quickening production. Then, too, both branches are turning out trained pilots, useful in national emergency, many of whom will eventually find their way into the fields of commercial aviation.

I can't help expressing the wish that men already trained could have more opportunity to fly. Many excellent flyers who served in the war, and later, want to keep in practise. They can, of course, join the reserves and fly Peteys (P.T.s), the training plane which replaced the Jennys, recently condemned. But flying a P.T. doesn't equip one to pilot the modern pursuit and larger planes. Unless these men are able to afford the luxuries of planes of their own, they can't obtain any adequate training and their great value in possible national emergency is lessened. Could they be permitted to fly new type planes that are in the army hangars, it would save all the lost motion of retaining them in time of need, besides keeping them interested.

Probably no department of aviation touches the business people of the country more closely than the air mail, which, by the way, includes not only letters but express and freight as well. The Aircraft Year Book analysis of the activities of the Post Office Department is so admirable I again quote from it verbatim:

"The Post Office Department, relieved of the details of the actual operations of flying the mail through letting out this work at public bidding to private operators, has been devoting its efforts exclusively under the direction of Second Assistant Postmaster General W. Irving Glover, to the building up of the network of privately operated air mail lines and of bringing to the attention of the public the value of the air mail service.

"One of the high lights in the operation of the air

mail service in 1927 was the splendid demonstration by this service of the safety of commercial operations with able pilots, good equipment and efficient ground organization, under most trying flying conditions. This is attested by the Post Office Department's record last year of a single fatality in 1,413,381 miles of day and night air transportation.

"Another achievement was the steady increase in the use of the air mail by the public. This is shown by the fact that while the mileage flown by private mail route operators was practically the same in June, 1926, as in June, 1927, the amount of mail carried by these private lines had increased from 29,673 pounds in June, 1926, to 55,026 pounds in June, 1927. Another measure of the increase in the use of the air mail service is found in the Government figures showing that while the number of miles flown in carrying mail during the first half of 1927 was practically the same as the mileage flown in the last half of the year, the compensation to the operators which is based on the poundage carried, had increased nearly 50 per cent. The Government figures show that while the average revenue per mile to operators during the first half of 1927 was 58.4 cents, it had jumped to 76.9 cents during the last half of the year.

"A third notable accomplishment of the Post Office Department in 1927 was the success of its night flying, which has led it to authorize a considerable additional mileage of night mail carrying by private

operators. The overnight operations now in effect
and to be put into effect as speedily as the additional
air mail routes are lighted, aggregate approximately
2,800,000 miles per year. The night flying program
includes the following services each night of the year:

Miles

Chicago, ILL., to RockSprings,Wyo..........1,100
Boston, Mass., to New York.....................192
Chicago,ILL., to Dallas, Texas...................987
Cleveland, Ohio, to Louisville, Ky..............339
New York to Atlanta..............................773
3,391

"This night flying, formerly done by the Post
Office Department, but now relinquished entirely to
private mail transport companies, aggregates more
than a million and three-quarter miles of flying in the
year, and constitutes the greatest night air flying operation in the world."

In the development of aviation—especially long
distance flying, and pioneer over-water efforts—meteorological study is vital. In connection with the
Friendship flight I have told somewhat of how its backers cooperated in supplementing the work of the
Weather Bureau with separately collected data. These
efforts brought home to us all, I am sure, a vivid
realization of how much is to be done in that field—
a need understood better by no one than the weather
experts themselves.

Our knowledge of Atlantic weather is extraordinarily incomplete. Generally speaking, the machinery for securing the requisite data actually exists, but there are not funds to pay for its utilization. The Weather Bureau has no appropriation to meet the costs of the constant reports that should be radioed in by ships at sea, if the Bureau is to be able to forecast with accuracy precise detail conditions prevailing in various areas.

Meteorologists tell me, for instance, that if reports at intervals of say every four hours could be secured from vessels between America and Europe, much, if not all, of the uncertainty regarding trans-Atlantic weather conditions as they affect air travel could be avoided. Shortly, it seems probable, Congress will provide funds for such work. Possibly even an international code will be created, with the cooperation of the steamship companies themselves, so that supplying such data will be automatic. At present, providing it is purely a matter of individual accommodation, and the person getting it has to pay the transmission bills which are likely to be heavy.

Reports six times daily, say from a hundred different vessels, would permit experts on both sides of the Atlantic to lay out weather charts of incalculable value. The information sent would primarily include barometric pressure, temperature, wind direction and velocity and visibility.

Ultimately the exact position of storms and their

movements will be determinable. With such information the fast-flying sturdy airships of the future
can set their courses so as to avoid these storms, and
to take advantage of favorable flying conditions.

CHAPTER 13

RETROSPECT

PREPARATIONS...THE FLIGHT...England...our return... the first receptions...photographs, interviews...New York, Boston, Chicago...the many invitations not accepted because of lack of time...mayors, celebrities, governors...splendid flyers; Wilkins, Byrd, Chamberlin, Thea Rasche, Balchen, Ruth Nichols, Reed Landis... speeches, lunches, radio microphones...acres of clippings (unread)...editors, promoters...settlement houses, aldermen's offices...gracious hostesses, camera-wise politicians...private cars, palatial planes...and then my book...hours of writing piled up in the contented isolation (stoically maintained) of a hospitable Rye home...friends, a few parties...swimming, riding, dancing, in tantalizing driblets...brief recesses from work...Tunney vs. Heeney, my first fight (a boxer's career is measured by minutes in the ring; an aviator's by hours in the air)...more writing—much more.

EARHART IN THE *FRIENDSHIP*

Such is my jumbled retrospect of the seven weeks which have crowded by since we returned to America.

Finally the little book is done, such as it is. Tomorrow I am free to fly.

Now, I have checked over, from first to last, this manuscript of mine. Frankly, I'm far from confident of its air-worthiness, and don't know how to rate its literary horse-power or estimate its cruising radius and climbing ability. Confidentially, it may never even make the take-off.

If a crash comes, at least there'll be no fatalities. No one can see more comedy in the disaster than the author herself. Especially because even the writing of the book, like so much else of the flight and its after-maths, has had its humor—some of it publishable!

I never knew that a "public character" (that, Heaven help me, apparently is my fate since the flight) could be the target of so much mail.

"Please send me $150; it will just pay for my divorce which I must have...." So read one letter, plus details anent the necessity of the proposed separation. Autographing, I discover, is a national mania. Requests for photographs, freak suggestions, involved communications from inventors, pathetic appeals, have been numerous.

Yes, the mail has brought diverse proposals of marriage, and approximations thereof. Perhaps the widespread publication of my photograph has kept the quantity down!

Best of all the letters are those from average people about the country—mostly women—who have found
some measure of satisfaction, or perhaps a vicarious
thrill, in the experiment of which I happened to be a
small part. For their congratulations and friendly
messages I find myself always deeply grateful.

A wave of invitations almost engulfed me, and offers
of employment, many of them bewilderingly generous,
proved part of the harvest of notoriety. The psychology
of inferring that flying the Atlantic equips one for an
advertising managership or banking, leaves me puzzled.

However, the correspondence of a "goldfish" isn't
all bouquets, by any means.

Cigarettes have nearly been my downfall. Not sub-
jectively, understand, for my indulgence is decently limited; the count, I think, shows the restrained total of
three for the current year. It's not what I did, but
what I said, that caused trouble. I wickedly "endorsed"
a certain cigarette which was carried by the boys on the
Friendship. This I did to benefit three gallant gentlemen,—
Commander Byrd, to whose South Polar Expedition
I turned over my own financial proceeds, and the
companions on my flight who benefited only if my name
was used. Among the immediate souvenirs of my
viciousness is a copy of the advertisement, torn from
a newspaper and sent to me by an irate commentator.
On the margin she wrote: "I suppose you drink too!"

It happens that I don't—it just never seemed
worth while. Anyway, the incident struck some jour-

nalistic sparks. Amusing among them is this from the "New Yorker":

O NE of the greatest personal sacrifices of all times, as we look at it, was the sacrifice Miss Earhart made in endorsing a brand of cigarettes so she could earn fifteen hundred dollars to contribute to Commander Byrd's South Pole flight. She admitted in her letter that she "made the endorse-

ment deliberately." Commander Byrd, replying, said that it seemed to him "an act of astonishing generosity." Pioneering must go on, whatever the toll; the waste places must be conquered. Since, however, the faculty of Reed University, in Oregon, declares that it is impossible for a person blindfolded to tell one cigarette from another, it seems to us that the only honorable course left for Commander Byrd, in order to vindicate science and validate Miss Earhart's gift, is to fly to the South Pole blindfolded.

Photographers, too, are innocent (sometimes) instruments of a critical fate. (I've never fathomed why photographers always want "a-great-big-smile-please"; and prefer their victims waving.) I did contrive to resist the blandishments of one who would have had me pictured blowing a kiss to Pittsburgh. But in Chicago, when the boys and girls of the Hyde Park High School turned out to see their Atlantic-flying Alumna, the picture men asked me to step forward from the stage upon a grand piano backed up to its edge, so as to include the youngsters as well as myself. Picture taken, pictured published. Promptly arrived an acid letter from a friend: "*How* did you get on the piano?"

Doubtless she visualized me in scandalizing progress through the west, leaping from piano to piano.

The school incident reminds me of my peripatetic education. My father was a railroad claim agent and attorney, his work seldom keeping him long in one place. As a result I graced the high schools of six different communities, and happened to be in Chicago when graduation day rolled around. During the first turmoil after our London arrival, cablegrams came from at least four communities, each one doing me the honor of claiming me as its very own. Beyond proclaiming the fact that I spent more time in Atchison, Kansas, than anywhere else, discretion, it seems to me, dictates silence as to other comparative allegiances.

A considerable crop of poetry, verse, and rhyme is chargeable to our flight, some of it far more meritorious than the subject sung. From the direct-by-mail offering, with which friendly souls seem wont to deluge those whose names appear in print, I garner the following excerpts:

> The men were anxious, Amelia was too,
> Still they never lost hope, just flew and flew.
> It took great courage, for a flight like that,
> And to the girl Amelia, we take off our hat.

> She's my Amelia, the darling of the air,
> She sailed for Europe without a thought or a care,
> Just to let the world know that a girl could bring
> To the U. S. A. fame and most every other thing.

Two experiences which were privileges, too, of the busy weeks, stand out oddly in my memory.

Shamelessly I confess my admiration for motor-cycle policemen. Though they have spoken harshly to me on occasion they are so good to look at, I've quite forgiven—most of them. Gallant figures cycle cops, weaving through traffic, provoking drivers to follow suit—and get a ticket.

In the autocratic days of our post-flight glory we were whirled about with motorcycle escort, unmindful of traffic lights and speed ordinances. Of an afternoon I motored to New York's new Medical Center, with one of the escorts driving a side-car. On the way back to the Biltmore I transferred from the limousine to that side-car....There wasn't a speedometer so I don't know exactly, but I suspect that fifty m.p.h. doesn't tell the story.

That was one of the cherished experiences. The second found me in a locomotive cab of the Pennsylvania Railroad, bedecked in overalls, goggles and cap. The ride from Pittsburgh to Altoona, round the Horseshoe Bend, was not so fast as flying, about as noisy, and much dirtier. Also far more hot. If and when my feminine readers take up locomotive travel, let them wear heavily soled shoes. Mine were fairly thin—and the fire box heated the floor below where I sat when I couldn't stand and stood when I couldn't sit. Even the photographs, incidental to these experiences, did not detract from my enjoyment. However, some of them clipped subsequently from newspapers, arrived thoughtfully labelled *bologna*.

There were many editorials in both England and America. Some appraised the technical accomplishments of the flight generously. But more interesting than the bouquets were the brickbats, especially when shied directly at me—as they often were.

As to the part I personally played in the flight I have tried to be entirely frank always. The credit belongs to the boys, to the ship and to its backer. I was a passenger. The fact that I happened to be a small-ship pilot, reasonably experienced in the air, didn't affect the situation other than having contributed to my selection.

Said the "New York World":

Using Newfoundland and Ireland, and possibly the Azores, as fuel stops, commercial airplaning between the Old World and the New appears likely to become

feasible within the not very distant future. To have
shared with her skilled companions in bringing that
development a step nearer is higher honor for Miss
Earhart than the sporting record of the first air crossing accomplished by a woman.

Not only "honor," but satisfaction—the joy of a
share, however small, in a great adventure.

When we were in London a clipping from "The
Church Times" came to me. The envelope was
addressed in the shaky handwriting of an elderly person. There was no letter and no signature, but certain
sentences in the article were underlined.

Here is that clipping as it greeted me, the underlined sentences printed in italics:

READ MARK LEARN

A young American woman has crossed the
Atlantic in an aeroplane and has arrived
safely on the shore of Wales. Within the
past few months three other women have
lost their lives in attempting the same
feat, and Miss Earhart is to be congratulated on escaping their fate. The voyage
itself, for nearly all the way through fog,
is a remarkable achievement made possible by the skill
and courage of the pilot. But his anxiety must have
been vastly increased by the fact that he was
carrying a woman passenger, and, as the
"Evening Standard" has properly pointed

out, *her presence added no more to the achievement than if the passenger had been a sheep.* [This is the zoological last straw! After two weeks of mutton at Trepassey I'm sure the boys could not have endured the proximity of a sheep as cargo on the *Friendship.*] Miss Earhart has been acclaimed by Welsh villagers, congratulated by Mr. Coolidge, lionized in London, and she is offered large sums of money to appear in the films. For us, it is all a rather pitiful commentary on "so-called civilization." Society cannot profit directly or indirectly from Miss Earhart's journey. *She is an international heroine simply and solely because, owing to good luck and an airman's efficiency,* she is the first woman to travel from America to Europe by air. A scientist has died after many years of agony because of his devotion to the work of healing, and for him there are only brief paragraphs in the newspapers, while Miss Earhart has columns. Women suffer constant discomfort and risk infection from loathsome diseases, working for the unhappy in slums, in leper colonies, in the fetid tropics, and their names remain unknown. *Certainly, the sense of values in the modern world is sadly distorted.*

For compensation, here is another clipping, a chuckling commentary upon back-seat driving, of course utterly unfair to my sex:

AS A BACK SEAT DRIVER WOULD HAVE
MADE THAT FLIGHT

(Two Hundred Miles off Trepassey.)

The Woman: Where are we now?

Pilot: I can't quite make out.

The Woman: There must be some way of telling.

Pilot: I just don't seem to recognize anything.

The Woman: Are you sure that place we left was Trepassey?

Pilot: That's what it was called on the map.

The Woman: Well, maybe the map was wrong. I don't feel as if we were headed for Europe. Hadn't we better stop and make certain?

* * *

(One Thousand Miles Out.)

The Woman: Are we on the right route now?

Navigator: I'm pretty certain, but I wouldn't swear to it.

The Woman: I'll bet we're miles off going ahead blindly if we're not certain!

Pilot: We may be a little off the course.

The Woman: I'll bet we're miles off it. I could have told you 600 miles back we weren't going the right way. Can't you straighten things out by looking at the map?

Navigator: The map won't do us any good just now.

The Woman: What's a map for, then? I'll bet if I had a map I could tell where I was.

(Twelve Hundred Miles Out.)

The Woman: Why do we have to keep flying in this awful fog? It's perfectly terrible!

Pilot: There's no way of avoiding it.

The Woman: That's a perfectly silly thing to say. When you sail right into a fog and stay in it for hours I should think you'd admit you'd made a mistake and not drive calmly on, pretending it was necessary.

Pilot: We've flown way up in the air to get out of it and we've flown close to the ocean to escape it, but it's no use.

The Woman: I'll bet if you'd turn a sharp right you'd get out of it in no time. I told you to take a sharp right five hours ago.

Pilot: We can't take any sharp right turns and reach Europe, my dear.

The Woman: How do you know without trying?

* * *

(Fifteen Hundred Miles Out.)
The Woman: Well, I just know we're lost and it's all your fault.
Navigator: Please have a heart. Everything'll come out okay if you have patience.
The Woman: I've had patience for hours, and for all I know may be right back where I started. If you don't know exactly where you are why don't you STOP AND ASK SOMEBODY?

* * *

(Over South Wales.)
The Woman: Look! It's land! What place is it?
Pilot: The British Isles.
The Woman: Isn't it just splendid? Here we are across the Atlantic in no time just as we had planned. And you boys were so NERVOUS AND UNCERTAIN ABOUT IT ALL THE WAY OVER!

H. I. Phillips added that to the gaiety of aviation, in the Sun Dial of the "New York Sun." By the way, at the N. A. A. luncheon at the Boston reception I was introduced as the most famous b. s. d. in the world.

One of the largest organizations connected with the *Friendship* flight was the I-knew-all-about-it-before-hand-club. Most of them contrived to get into the papers pretty promptly. Some charter members recorded that they turned down tempting offers to pilot the ship, actuated by an exuberant loyalty to Uncle Sam.

Here, in conclusion of this hodge-podge are three more extracts from the press, random examples of what men do and say.

The first is from the "English Review," evidence that the world is far from any universal air-mindedness:

The Latest Atlantic Flight

The Atlantic has been flown again, and no one will grudge Miss Earhart her triumph. The achievement has, however, produced the usual crop of inspired paragraphs on the future of aviation, and the usual failure to face the fact that air transport is the most unreliable and the most expensive form of transport available. No amount of Atlantic flights will alter these facts, because they happen, as things are, to be inherent in the nature of men and things. Absurd parallels are drawn between people who talk sense about the

air today, and people who preferred stage-
coaches to railways. The only parallel
would be, of course, between such people and any who insist today in flying to
Paris by balloon instead of by aeroplane.
Everyone wants to see better, safer and
cheaper aeroplanes. If the Air League
can offer us a service which will take us to
Paris in half-an-hour for half-a-crown,
I would even guarantee that Neon would
be the first season-ticket holder. But all
this has nothing to do with the essential
fact that not a single aeroplane would be
flying commercially today without the
Government subsidy, for the simple reason that by comparison with other forms
of transport air transport is uneconomic.
To talk vaguely of the great developments
which will occur in the future is no answer,
unless you can show that the defects of air
transport are technical defects which can
be overcome by mechanical means. A few
of them, of course, are, but the over-
whelming defects are due to the nature of
the air itself. It is very unfortunate, but
we fail to see how it can be helped.

After all, the "Review" may be right; but somehow its
viewpoint is reminiscent of certain comment when the

Wrights were experimenting at Kitty Hawk. Also of the mathematical deductions which proved beyond doubt that flight in a heavier than air machine was impossible.

To balance the pessimism here is an editorial from this morning's "New York Times"—current commentary upon characteristic news of the day:

Steamship and Plane

In the world of commerce a gain of fifteen hours in the receipt of letters from Europe may have important consequences. The experiment of the French Line was to be only a beginning in speeding Atlantic mails. It is yet planned to launch planes when steamships are 800 miles from the port of destination. With a following wind the amphibian plane piloted by Commander Demougeot flew at the rate of 130 miles an hour and made the distance of over 400 miles to Quarantine in three hours and seventeen minutes. In such weather as prevailed it could have been catapulted from the Ile de France with no more hazard when she was 800 miles away, or about one-fourth of the distance between Havre and New York.

Ten years ago the experiment of hurrying mail to shore in a plane from a surface ship 400 miles out at sea would

not have been attempted. So great has
been the improvement in airplane design
that what the Ile de France has done will
soon become the regular order. It is not
wildly speculative to think of dispatching
a plane after a liner on a well-traveled
route in these days of excellent radio
communication. It would be well to use
for that purpose amphibian or seaplanes
carrying fuel enough to take them all the
way across the Atlantic if necessary.

It is conceivable that ocean flight
between Europe and the United States
will be the sequel to a ship-and-plane
system of mail delivery, the distances
covered by the plane becoming longer and
longer until the steamship can be dis-
pensed with altogether.

And last, just an item of news, gleaned from "Time":

BROKER'S AMPHIBIAN
Between his summer home on Buzzard's
Bay, Mass., and his brokerage offices in
Manhattan, Richard F. Hoyt commutes
at 100 miles an hour. He uses a Loening
amphibian biplane, sits lazily in a cabin
finished in dark brown broadcloth and
saddle leather, with built-in lockers con-

taining pigskin picnic cases. Pilot Robert
E. Ellis occupies a forward cockpit,
exposed to the breezes. But occasionally
Broker Hoyt wishes to pilot himself. When
this happens he pulls a folding seat out of
the cabin ceiling, reveals a sliding hatch.
Broker Hoyt mounts to the seat, opens the
hatch, inserts a removable joystick in a
socket between his feet. Rudder pedals
are already installed in front of the folding seat. He has thus created a rear cockpit, with a full set of controls. Broker
Hoyt becomes Pilot Hoyt.

With such excerpts, from the newspapers and the
magazines of every day, one could go on endlessly, for
aviation is woven ever closer into the warp of the
world's news. Ours is the commencement of a flying
age, and I am happy to have popped into existence at
a period so interesting.

WILMER STULTZ—Pilot

Born April 11, 1900.

He enlisted in 1917 for the duration of the war. Joined
the 634th Aero Squadron at San Antonio, Texas, and
later served at Middletown, Pa. Discharged March, 1919.

On August 4, 1919, married Mildred Potts, of
Middletown.

December 2, 1919, Stultz joined the Navy, being stationed at Hampton Roads, Virginia, until July, 1920. Then he went to Pensacola, Florida, to the flight school, where he received training with seaplanes, in the ground school, and in navigation, aerology, meteorology, radio, etc. Thereafter he returned to Hampton Roads until December 2, 1922, securing his discharge.

In February, 1923, Stultz took a position with Curtiss Export Company, being sent to Rio de Janeiro to oversee the setting up of forty F5L and other types of planes. He also instructed Brazilians in flying. That autumn he returned to New York, working with the Curtiss Company at Curtiss Field. Later for the Fokker Company he tested the "Josephine Ford" used by Commander Byrd.

Among those for whom he flew subsequently were Al Pack, President of the Hubbard Steel Foundries, for the Gates Flying Circus, and the Reynolds Airways.

In August Stultz joined Mrs. Grayson, testing her plane, "The Dawn." From Old Orchard, Maine, in October he made three take-off attempts with Mrs. Grayson. A flight of about 500 miles was terminated by engine trouble. Lacking confidence in the "Dawn's" equipment, he severed his connection with Mrs. Grayson.

In November, 1927, Stultz took a position with Arrow Airways, Paterson, N. J., which he left to make flights with Charles Levine to Havana, etc.

Thereafter he became associated with the *Friendship* flight.

LOUIS EDWARD GORDON—Flight Mechanic

Born March 4, 1901, San Antonio, Texas.

Gordon enlisted in the Army Air Service at Ellington Field, Houston, Texas, July 15, 1919.

Later he was transferred to the 20th Bombing Squadron and went to Kelly Field, San Antonio, Texas, where he had six months in the aircraft motor school. Rejoining his organization in New York, he was assigned as mechanic to two tri-motored Caproni and one Handley Page plane. In May, 1921, he was with the Handley Page bombers during operations against obsolete battleships off the Virginia Capes.

Subsequently Gordon became Chief Mechanic at the proving grounds, Aberdeen, Maryland. Then until 1926 he served with bombers at Mitchell Field, where he was throughout the International Air Races. In May, 1926, after seven years and nine days in the service, he received his honorable discharge as Staff Sergeant.

Gordon next was with the Philadelphia Rapid Transit Air Service, operating Fokker tri-motors between Philadelphia, Washington, and Norfolk.

In June, 1927, R. J. Reynolds bought the ships. Gordon was working on a tri-motor at Monroe, Louisiana, when Stultz, telephoning from New York, asked him if he would like to join up on the *Friendship* project. The next day he met Stultz in Detroit and joined the *Friendship*.

On July 20, 1928, he married Ann Bruce of Brookline, Mass.